# ᴀMINDFUL EVENING

DAVID DILLARD-WRIGHT, PD

# *A* MINDFUL EVENING

### Complete each day with a calm mind and open heart

AVON, MASSACHUSETTS

Published by
Adams Media, a division of F+W Media, Inc.
57 Littlefield Street, Avon, MA 02322. U.S.A.
www.adamsmedia.com

ISBN 10: 1-4405-9867-3
ISBN 13: 978-1-4405-9867-8
eISBN 10: 1-4405-9868-1
eISBN 13: 978-1-4405-9868-5

Printed in China.

10 9 8 7 6 5 4 3 2 1

The information in this book should not be used for diagnosing or treating any health problem. Not all diet and exercise plans suit everyone. You should always consult a trained medical professional before starting a diet, taking any form of medication, or embarking on any fitness or weight-training program. The author and publisher disclaim any liability arising directly or indirectly from the use of this book.

Many of the designations used by manufacturers and sellers to distinguish their products are claimed as trademarks. Where those designations appear in this book and F+W Media, Inc. was aware of a trademark claim, the designations have been printed with initial capital letters.

*This book is available at quantity discounts for bulk purchases.*
*For information, please call 1-800-289-0963.*

For the victims of violence and their families.

•

# Contents

8
•

# Acknowledgments

Sincere thanks to Eileen Mullan, Laura Daly, and the whole team at F+W/Adams Media for the beautiful work on this book and *A Mindful Morning*. Jessica Dillard-Wright provided encouragement through the hard work of writing these books. Thanks to the Dillard and Wright families for your support. Thanks to Jane Stafford and John Black for the speaking opportunities that helped to clarify my thinking. Thanks to Natalia Bowdoin and Sabrina MisirHiralall for friendship and conversation and to the USC Aiken community for ten good years.

# Introduction

The sun hangs low in the western sky, leaves silhouetted against the golden expanse. Cars, finally freed from the stranglehold of snarled traffic, make their way to houses and apartments. Evening has come, and with it the promise of food and rest. The day's labors draw to a close. Sleep may be hours away, but something has definitely changed. The rhythm of life slows and the edges of things soften as the moon rises. The moon—emblem of devotion, counterpart to the sun's harsh truth—can be seen hanging low in the sky. With the moon comes the stars, the opening of the heavenly maps to other worlds, to other places on this blue orb. With night comes the chance to forget, to dream, to escape, and yet it is still evening. Evening, like dawn, is the in-between. Unlike dawn, the evening is the waning of the powers of day, the last vestige of the tracings of the hours, a diagram half erased. What transpired this day now lies in the past, already become memory—a wisp of smoke, a reverberation.

Welcome to *A Mindful Evening*, a treasury of wisdom and exploration, a chance to delve deep inside and explore at the close of day. This book helps you to put a period (or at least an ellipsis) on the events that have taken place in your life over the last twenty-four hours. It helps you to close the loop, close the cycle on the joyous or tumultuous occurrences that have occupied your time and attention in this, the latest sojourn through the changing world. This is the exhalation of the day, the last breath of the mini death that we experience each night. In the cycle of seasons, the evening is the autumn, the prelude to the winter of night. In the notes of a chord, it is the fifth, which makes for completion. On the fingers of the hand, it is the ring finger, the done deal, the already committed. Evening can be tinged with joy or regret, blessings counted or curses lamented. Evening is a milestone and a passage, however brief.

The evening is traditionally a time for prayer—the Islamic *al-Maghrib*, Jewish *Maariv*, Christian vespers, Hindu *sandhyā*—but it is also a time for feasting and drinking. The evening is the most spiritual and most worldly time of day, the second great transition that takes place each solar cycle. For the pious, it is a time for protection from the demonic forces; for the impious, it is the true dawn. Evening holds great tension and even contradiction: It is the balance of opposing forces, the fulcrum of life, the point between systole and diastole. Whether fast or festival, it speaks of closing. It whispers of drying leaves, of fragility and entropy. It wears the same colors as dawn, but more garishly, as though the day had grown conscious of its age and decided to flaunt it.

# Winding Down

We have a pernicious tendency to judge ourselves at the close of day. Nagging questions linger, perhaps on the drive home, while sitting at dinner, or lying down to sleep at night. "Did I accomplish enough today? Did I pay the bills? Was I good enough as a partner or employee or parent?" This analysis has the potential to spiral out of control, to become fodder for insomnia, to lead to chronic stress. The little annoyances of daily life can be magnified out of proportion, making Mount Rushmores out of molehills. Notice that if we have been engaged in work, the activities likely to be labeled as "productive" by our society, we have a tendency to criticize ourselves in the opposite direction. So we might ask questions related to self-care, like, "Did I eat well enough today? Did I do my meditation? Did I start writing my novel?" So there is a Catch-22 of self-regulating thought. We can criticize ourselves for being too "worldly" or too "spiritual," for being too obsessed with success or for not being successful enough. We need to develop techniques of self-inquiry that do not become a sort of torture session where we castigate ourselves for everything that we did not accomplish over the previous day.

One beneficial practice is to have boundary rituals where we mark the transition from one phase of the day to another. I remember the old *Mister Rogers' Neighborhood* episodes, where that smiling 1960s gentleman would change out of his work blazer and into his play cardigan, out of his work shoes and into his sneakers. Mr. Rogers was getting ready for his imagination time. I don't have the same extensive library of cardigan sweaters as Mr. Rogers, but I usually do take off my shoes and at least change shirts when I come home from work. Sleep experts usually recommend keeping electronic devices out of the bed and having a buffer between "screen time" and sleep time. I confess that I am not as good about that, and I tend to read a good bit before sleep. I do notice that sometimes the stimulation of the Internet or streamed programming makes for less sleep. In some cases, the screen time may be worthwhile, and at other times it may just be killing time that could be better spent asleep.

In an ideal world, we would all do some chanting and/or meditation each night, but it can be difficult to work into a hectic routine. Dinner has to be made and the dishes cleaned. Even ordering take-out requires a modicum of effort and cleanup. Animals, whether dogs, cats, parakeets, or boa constrictors, must be fed and watered. Families with children must make sure the homework is done and that the kids are fed and bathed. The laundry takes a good bit of daily effort. Oftentimes, adults have homework as well, maybe a report to be read or written, maybe a writing project. Finally, after all of that is done, it is quite understandable that most people just want to relax by watching a movie or television program.

The exercises in this book are designed to be short, requiring only a few minutes, so that you can work them into your routine, no matter how busy that routine might be. If you have five or ten minutes each evening, as distraction-free as possible, you can fully complete all of the exercises in this book. If you have more time, you can add more silent meditation, or perhaps read some scripture or philosophy.

You might be able to take a quick pause right when you walk in the door in the evening, or it might be right before closing your eyes to sleep. Try to get into a routine if you can, but don't beat yourself up if you miss a day, or even a week. Don't allow your mindfulness practice to become just one more form of self-criticism. Meditation should be one way that you can love yourself and take care of yourself. And when I say "love," I don't mean the selfish, shallow sort of self-love. I mean the deep lovingkindness that sees past faults and forgives past wrongs. I mean unconditional, divine love. We are all capable of extending this love to ourselves, and through this process we heal the deep wounds of the past. As we begin to heal ourselves of the disappointments and heartbreaks of the past, we become more able to move confidently into the future. We also become more ready and willing to love others, as our defenses become less necessary and we become more open-hearted. The paradox of self-love and self-care is that such daily disciplines make us more available to others, and we do not just engage in the practices for ourselves.

Transformation doesn't happen overnight, in the sense that changing habits that have taken a lifetime to accrue will not automatically yield to a new way of being. But change does happen overnight in the sense that the thoughts that you put into your head before sleep carry over into the quality of rest and the thoughts that you have upon awaking the next day. The mind that is constantly going, constantly chewing on something, will eventually produce mental and physical health problems. The inability to cope with stress has real repercussions for your health and your society's. By practicing mindfulness and meditation before sleep, you avoid carrying yesterday's garbage into tomorrow. You leave the problems of this day behind and allow yourself to make a fresh start. You allow the day to come to a close, not just temporally but existentially as well. You make peace with the day, no matter how well or how badly it has gone, and let go of it. You put the day to bed as you put yourself to bed.

# Beginning, Middle, and End

Aristotle, in the *Poetics*, said that a good tragedy must have a beginning, a middle, and an end. The plot has a setup, a climax, and a denouement, and much the same can be said of any plot arc in fiction. A good novel has many such arcs: a large one with many smaller ones nested underneath that in the various subplots. We all hope that our lives are not tragedies or tragicomedies, but we all do have a beginning, middle, and end to our lives. We just don't know which phase applies at any given time. We don't know exactly how or when life will end, but the end comes for all of us. Each day is a microcosm, a tiny subplot of this larger story that we tell while living our lives. Evening is a time for making peace with the day, for saying goodbye to all of the dramatis personae of the day's events, the sadness and joy that has taken place.

The fact that this lifetime ends does not have to be viewed as a bad thing. Even if the end of life brings sorrow, we hope that it is a sweet sorrow. If we have done all that we came to earth to do, if we have done our best by our loved ones, if we have made each day count, there will be no reason for regret. The shortness and fragility of life makes it valuable. Whether you think that we go through many hundreds, if not thousands, of lifetimes or whether you believe we only get the one chance, this day is a unique experience. By greeting this evening mindfully, on this day, we prepare for the evening of life, when everything will be said and done. By making peace with this day, we make peace with life in general.

In the Hindu tradition, one of the five observances (*niyamas*) is called *santosha*, contentment. I like the idea of *santosha* as a practice, because we usually think of contentment as something attained by rearranging external circumstances. In other words, we usually say, "I'll be content once I make *x* salary, once I get *y* promotion, once I have *z* level of education." This, of course, leads to a never-ending hamster wheel effect, in which contentment never actually comes. The idea behind *santosha* is to do quite the opposite, to be purposely content with wherever my life might be right now, to just accept my lot, whatever my lot might be. That might sound like fatalism or resignation, but there is a subtle difference. *Santosha* is not grim stoicism: It is meeting life with joy and courage. It is very hard for naturally melancholic people, but it is the remedy for persistent feelings of lack and self-doubt.

So the evening can be a good time for practicing *santosha*. Everyone has different ways of winding down. Some people like to talk through the day's events with a friend or partner; other people just want some peace and quiet. Regardless of whether you are more introverted or extroverted, there may be times when you don't get to go through your desired regimen. Ideally, we would all have time for chanting and meditation at the close of day, but maybe your situation doesn't allow for that. The exercises in this book will allow you to have a very simple ritual to close your day that doesn't involve a lot of planning.

# How to Use This Book

This book is designed to be read one entry per day. Each entry has a quote, a reflection, and an exercise. You can choose for yourself how formal you want to be with the practice. If you like, you can light a candle and burn some incense, or use this book as part of your existing meditation practice. You can also be less formal and just keep this book by the bed or on your e-reader. You could also read the entry at your evening meal, either individually or with your family or community. A wide range of philosophies and traditions are represented in the quotes: Anyone, regardless of background or degree of religiosity, can benefit from mindfulness practice.

You will naturally gravitate toward some of the exercises more than others. Perhaps one of these quotes catches you at exactly the right time. Perhaps one of the exercises matches exactly with your life circumstances. Just be aware that even if something rubs you the wrong way, that doesn't mean it is wrong for you. Sometimes we need to be pushed into uncomfortable places, as that is really where the growth occurs. Stick with the practice even and especially if it becomes tedious or boring. In those moments of spiritual dryness, we push past our former boundaries and move into new frontiers of awareness.

Sometimes we abandon a practice just when it starts working. It's kind of like when you get sick and go on a course of antibiotics.

The temptation is to stop taking the drug as soon as you feel better. Of course, the right thing to do is to complete the course, as this prevents resistant strains from developing. So it goes with spiritual practice and with this book: Try to finish it even if you begin to feel better, even if you feel like it is old hat. Marathon runners talk about hitting the wall at around mile eighteen, and so it goes with any spiritual discipline. In the words of Sri Sai Baba of Shirdi, a certain amount of *shraddha* and *saburi* (patience) is necessary in order for the divine consciousness to bloom. Jacob had to wrestle the angel before he received a blessing (Genesis 32:22–31). In the *Ramayana*, Rama had to go into the wilderness and fight a great war before returning triumphant to Ayodhya.

I don't mean to scare you here: Rama and Sita also had some of their most peaceful times while exiled in the forest. You will find blooms here and not just thorns, but you can't have the blooms without the thorns. The paradox of spirituality is that by facing up to the difficulties and the ugliness of life, we come to find peace and joy. By avoiding difficulties, by avoiding the nasty parts of our nature, we create suffering and delusion. So we seek to *see clearly*, which is easier said than done. It can only be achieved by daily practice, by the work of a lifetime. And that happens one day at a time.

If mindfulness practice is to become an integral part of our lives, we have to find a place for it where we live and work. *A Mindful Morn-*

*ing* and this companion volume, *A Mindful Evening*, give you bookends to your day, to help you approach things positively and wind down gracefully. As I stress many times, meditation will not solve all of the problems in your life, but it will help you see your place in the human condition, to meet challenges with a little less angst and a little more patience. Sometimes that small difference in perspective makes a very great distance over time. Meditation allows you to recalibrate your moral and emotional compasses that you need to navigate through life confidently. The tiny course corrections that happen during mindfulness practice can give you a respite from the frantic pace of life and give you a modicum of calm in a turbulent world.

# What Can Mindfulness Do for You?

All sorts of claims are made for mindfulness practice and meditation. Even though psychologists and neurologists with scientific training have been studying meditation for several decades, patiently identifying the physiology of meditative states, there is still very little standing in the way of unscrupulous teachers making fantastic claims. Perhaps you've heard that meditation can help you levitate, talk to alien civilizations, or commune with the denizens of Atlantis. Perhaps you can learn to walk through walls or cure cancer, all with the power of the mind. I am a sucker for a good story, and I have an inordinate affection for the paranormal and metaphysical. But I would say, though, that it makes sense to stick to the more moderate claims for meditation and mindfulness.

Even the moderate claims are still pretty exciting. Meditation can help you reduce chronic pain, deal with the harmful effects of stress, get better sleep, and fight depression and anxiety—all without taking a pill. It makes sense to take the best of both worlds, to glean from Eastern spirituality and yogic practices what you can while still going to see doctors trained in Western medicine. Meditation is an important part of any overall wellness program, and there is now enough empirical evidence to recommend it to almost anyone. The techniques are simple, and the benefits are substantial. The only remaining factor is finding the practice that fits into your lifestyle in the time available. Too much spiritual practice will interfere with other priorities, while too little will not produce the intended benefits.

The practices in this book will get you started, but eventually you will want to receive personalized instruction from a qualified teacher who knows you and your circumstances. You will want to embark on a program, perhaps one lasting several years, that will see you through the ups and downs of the spiritual life. Meditators run into the same problems that affect endurance athletes: Eventually the practice comes to seem extremely dry and lifeless, something akin to "hitting the wall" in marathon running. This is known as spiritual dryness, anhedonia, or the "dark night of the soul." Philosophical descriptions of this state exist in many of the world's religious traditions, and it can be very difficult to move through. The initial reaction is usually to just quit the practice, but this may eliminate the breakthrough that is just around the corner.

A guru or teacher is the "coach" who sees you through all kinds of difficulties along the way. Unlike a "life coach," a label that suggests an overarching concern with career success and material prosperity, a spiritual director or guru is concerned, first and foremost, with illumination. A true guru will not seek to rob the disciple of wealth, will not use techniques of psychological manipulation, and will not promise more than he or she can offer. The true guru-disciple relationship is not a bond that lasts only for a season or even just for a lifetime. The true bond between the disciple and guru lasts until the disciple has achieved liberation from rebirth, no matter how long that might take. It is fully appropriate for the disciple to perform acts of service and make small material offerings for the benefit of the lineage (*parampara*), but it is the exception rather than the norm that the disciple would renounce the material world entirely.

Think of this book as an on-ramp to the great highway of the spiritual life. There are many such on-ramps, too numerous to count, but they are not all equal. To shift the image a bit, one often hears the metaphor that there are many paths leading to the summit of the same mountain. This might be superficially true, but keep in mind that some paths are a lot longer than the others! One still needs a sense of direction as well as a certain stamina and enthusiasm for reaching the summit. The superior spiritual athlete will overcome any obstacle in the way and will find the summit no matter how rough a goat track he or she has to tread. The halfhearted aspirant will not find the summit even with a ski lift leading straight to the top! Of course, this is just a tired metaphor, but you get the point.

The good qualities must ultimately come from the heart of the devotee and not from an external authority figure. Those good qualities—of patience, perseverance, love, and kindness—are what we revere and want to cultivate. We can do that with the most esoteric mystical practices, or we can do that by smiling at a stranger. Either way, we should keep firmly in mind the goal of becoming better people: opening our hearts to other people, learning to endure hardships, and seeing the beauty in the world.

# Synchronize Your Mind

*Whatever harm a foe may do to a foe, or a hater to another hater,*
*a wrongly directed mind may do one harm far exceeding these.*

*The Buddha*

In my adopted hometown of Augusta, Georgia, crew teams practice their rowing on the Savannah River, and there will be the occasional regatta on a Saturday morning. Dozens of narrow boats, outfitted with oars, smoothly ply the water, each rower in tune with the calls of the coxswain at the stern. The 4th Street Bridge bears the graffiti of the various universities who have rowed there. I am always amazed at the strength and coordination of these rowers, and I know from some of my friends how hard these athletes work, rising before dawn to run, do exercises, and row. Besides the hard work, it is really the synchronization of the team that makes the sport work.

This evening, take a look at your thoughts as you gaze upon your internal "regatta." Are all of your thoughts working harmoniously with one another? Perhaps some of your thoughts are racing ahead, out of rhythm. Breathe into the errant thoughts, restraining them. Or perhaps some of your thoughts fall behind, as in despondent or depressive attitudes. Perhaps you can nudge these low thoughts and feelings forward. As you breathe deeply, synchronize thought and feeling, looking for complete coordination and harmony.

# Take the Good, Take the Bad

*When you begin to understand, when you have been able to free yourself from a notion, that is enlightenment. . . . Don't say that enlightenment is foreign to you. You know what it is.*

*Thich Nhat Hanh, Buddhist monk and peace activist*

If you have ever been on a long car ride, you know how good it feels to get out of the car, stretch your legs, and breathe the fresh air. Being cramped and confined gives rise to the pleasure of stretching and moving. The monotony of the highway gives rise to the pleasure of strolling even the most banal rest stop. So we go through many contrasts in life, and these contrasts keep things interesting.

The trouble comes when we preference one pole over the other, when we want pleasure without pain, entertainment without boredom, agreement without dissent. Reality will simply not allow us to have anything unmixed. This evening, as you look upon your mental landscape, see if some small part of yourself does not want the good without the bad. See if you can reach a place of acceptance, where you acknowledge the parts of your reality that you cannot change.

# Willing Yourself Into Calm

*Resolve to keep happy, and your joy and you shall
form an invincible host against difficulties.*

Helen Keller, author and activist

Settle into the much-deserved rest at the end of this day. Allow yourself to fade into the rhythms of this evening, whether you are chopping vegetables in the kitchen or folding a pile of laundry, whether you are listening to the sounds of traffic or the sounds of crickets. Release the tension between your brows and allow yourself to merge with your surroundings. Release any conflicts you may have had with your loved ones or associates. Release troubles and worry. Release physical pain—if not the pain itself then the thought process associated with it.

If you are having trouble letting go, try exhaling worry, tension, and doubt. Inhale relaxation, joy, and peace. Exercise your will to bring yourself into a more calm state of mind. Open yourself to the possibility of divine presence. It may help to visualize your chosen divinity or perhaps a wise elder who has guided you along life's path. Allow the confusion and stress to dissolve, and bring your awareness to your calm center.

# Become Rooted with Gravity

*The closer men [sic] live to the rhythms of nature, the greater
their stability, poise, and sense of oneness with life.*

*Scott Nearing, radical economist and organic farmer*

Note the difference between useful planning and preparation and useless worry and anxiety. Planning and preparation make things easier and more harmonious, while worry and anxiety only eat away at your inner resolve. Allow yourself to plan and prepare for tomorrow morning, maybe by making yourself a lunch or a snack. Maybe pick tomorrow's outfit. Do a few minutes of homework, but do not ruin your evening by dwelling excessively on a meeting that has not happened yet. Do not run imaginary scenarios of gloom and doom in your head.

Whether you are seated now or lying down, you can allow gravity to become the focal point of your meditation. Feel gravity rooting you to the earth, giving you a sense of security and comfort. Imagine gravity not just pulling down on your body but also pulling down on the troubling thoughts, taking them right out of your consciousness. Just be aware for a few minutes of that gentle, familiar tug that roots you in place.

# From Division Into Community

*We have all known the long loneliness and we have learned that the only solution is love and that love comes with community.*

Dorothy Day, journalist and activist

Our media and politics continually draw our minds into false dichotomies, of left and right, civilized and savage, conservative and progressive, east and west, and so forth. Things would be different if we imagined things in circles rather than opposing poles: Each point of view tends to fade into the others when taken to its logical conclusion. Hence libertarians and anarchists may be regarded as "right" and "left," but they are not far apart on many issues. In order to have peace in society, we have to somehow make room for serious disagreement without demonizing the other. We must open a welcoming space in our minds and hearts, which is far more difficult than seeing oneself as always having the correct point of view.

This evening, you may find yourself clinging to a strident point of view, perhaps as a result of a news story that you read or something a friend said on social media. You probably cannot and should not let go of your personal ethics and your political beliefs, but perhaps you can hold these ideologies in suspension for the time being. Allow your mind to enter into a space of not-knowing, of not having solutions, of not casting blame. Before you go to sleep this evening, enter into a space of equanimity in which you regard all people in the same light. Give yourself the freedom to not have to have the correct belief.

# Winding Down Worry

*Worry does not empty tomorrow of its sorrow.*
*It empties today of its strength.*

Corrie ten Boom, *Holocaust resister*

As if the burdens of life were not enough, the mind makes them heavier and more difficult by dwelling on them excessively. Temporary problems come to seem like permanent features of reality. The fleeting difficulty becomes insurmountable. The mind is skilled at detecting threats, but this feature of the mind is not easily unwound or put on pause. The human mind, a product of our hunter-gatherer ancestry, is geared toward survival, but most of us would like more out of life than just survival. We want to thrive, to grow into new challenges and experiences.

Halve your burdens by concentrating on the breath. Breathing deeply and steadily, with a tranquil mind, develops equipoise and calm. This evening, as you draw closer to your rest, let each passing moment draw you deeper into peace. Know that whatever has captured your mind will not last. Everything changes; everything passes away. By the time you close your eyes to sleep, you will have complete contentment. The morning will bring a fresh mindset and creative solutions to all of your difficulties.

*Worry*

DOES NOT EMPTY TOMORROW
OF ITS SORROW.

IT EMPTIES TODAY OF ITS

*Strength.*

—Corrie ten Boom,
Holocaust resister

# Consider the Good

*Unhappy is that Grandeur which makes us too great to be good;*
*and that Wit which sets us at a distance from true Wisdom.*

Mary Astell, English feminist philosopher

Most of what you take for granted will one day come to an end. This body will age. This mind, too, will falter. People will enter your life and then leave again, for better or worse. You will hang your hat in many different places and inhabit many different social and economic circumstances. So today is one spark flung from the all-consuming fire, one note in the eternal song, one ripple in the ever-widening circle of existence.

You cannot stop change, and you are forced, by virtue of having been born, to act in the world. You can only choose the character of your interactions with others and your surroundings. Take a few minutes to look within, at the prevailing currents of your thoughts and emotions. Breathing deeply from your heart center, make a choice at this hour to live for truth, justice, and peace. Decide this evening to not be carried away by the desire for pleasure and possessions. Make a silent vow to consider the good of all beings in everything you think, say, and do.

# Seeing the Prison Walls

*Beside the noble art of getting things done,*
*there is the nobler art of leaving things undone.*

Lin Yutang, Chinese writer, translator, linguist, and inventor

You may have someone in your life today who has dogmatic or extreme beliefs, who refuses to hear contrary opinions, who says and does hurtful things. Carefully reasoned arguments will do nothing to sway the beliefs of a doctrinaire and inflexible person. Taunts and insults equally have no effect, like arrows that miss the mark. You may even worsen the problem through confrontation. And yet it seems irresponsible to not confront fundamentalism in some way, whether that fundamentalism is religious, political, or economic in nature. You find yourself wanting to stand for your own beliefs and speak your own truth.

To understand the difficult person, you need to see how that person is also caught in a prison of his or her own making. You have to intuit the injuries that the person tries to hide with ideological armor. When you see that person as injured and damaged, you will be able to see how to avoid exacerbating the situation. See the hurting part of that person, and you will see how to speak and relate skillfully. This evening, resolve to understand before acting, to see how your enemies feel and think about the world.

# Getting Nature's Magic Back

*To be nobody but yourself in a world which is doing its best, night and day, to make you everybody else means to fight the hardest battle which any human being can fight; and never stop fighting.*

E.E. Cummings, poet

When I was a child, the pecan tree in the side yard was not just a tree; it was a welcome friend. Its shade provided shelter for swordfights and magical battles. We left it gifts of coins buried in the dirt; we poured it offerings of milk and honey. We tried to understand the language of its rustling leaves in the wind and read the signs of birds perched in its branches. The tree was more of a "she" than an "it," more of a person than an object.

All children, if they have had a decent childhood, have something of a reverence for nature. It is only as we enter into adulthood that the spark of wonder dies through excessive calculation and classification. We forget to take off our shoes and walk in the grass. The magic in the world dies and is replaced with a drab, gray fog. But we can get the magic back this evening by simply asking for it. This evening, invite wonder and play into your life; allow your imagination to run freely to what *might* be.

# Clearing the Fog

*I'm not afraid of storms, for I'm learning to sail my ship.*

Louisa May Alcott, American author

Deep inside your heart, there is some small part of yourself that already knows what to do. It knows how to get you out of your emotional or mental funk. It knows how to solve the problems that confront you right now. It knows everything, but it should in no way be confused with the rational mind, or, even worse, the personality. This inner something is the divine Self at the heart of all reality. It was never born, and it will never die. It lives in you, and it lives in every creature. Entrust yourself to this deathless One, and you will have peace.

Only the fog of daily stress prevents you from contacting the inner guide. As you breathe deeply this evening, exhale all of the worries of the day, and let your inhalation feed the divinity within. Let go of all doubt, and perceive the inner guide growing stronger with each breath. If persistent troubles remain, simply mention them to the inner Self. Then go to bed confidently, knowing that the solution will soon appear.

# Cultivating Gratitude

*Pursue some path, however narrow and crooked,*
*in which you can walk with love and reverence.*

*Henry David Thoreau, American transcendentalist author*

We often sweat the details of the day that has already passed, wondering if we said the right things, ate the right diet, did enough exercise, crossed enough items off the to-do list. The reality is that while each little detail has a significance of its own, very few of them are game changers. Concern yourself more with the *how* of your actions rather than the *what*. Try to do things in a caring, gentle manner, even if that means you don't get as much done in terms of quantity. Your business associates and your family will notice your *tone* more than they notice the *content* of what you do.

This evening, cultivate gratitude for what you have been able to do today. Ask for help for what remains undone. Detach from what has already passed, and open your mind and heart in expectation of a restful night that restores your body and soul. Know that your abilities, your labor, and your insight are enough, more than enough, to conquer any challenges in your life.

# Count Your Wealth

*Day by day, what you choose, what you think,*
*and what you do is who you become.*

*Heraclitus, pre-Socratic Greek philosopher*

Once a student stepped into my office, which measures about six feet by eight feet, and I said, "Welcome to my closet." And then he responded, "Yeah, a rich man's closet," while looking over my shelves full of books and my diplomas hanging on the wall. I thought this was very odd, because I had never considered myself rich by any stretch of the imagination. But as I thought more deeply, I thought about wealth as where we invest our time and attention, and I have certainly spent a great deal of time and attention on my studies. The ivory tower may have turned into something of a gilded stump in recent years, but it is still a privileged position to be educated.

This evening, think for a few minutes about where your own wealth lies. Instead of worrying that you don't have enough, give thanks for the areas in your life where you have been successful and prosperous. You don't have to think of something big or grandiose. Maybe you could express gratitude for a beautiful day or a good meal with a friend. Quiet your inner curmudgeon with a few quiet words of thanks before going to bed tonight.

# Playing Like You Mean It

*The best way out is always through.*

Robert Frost, American poet

If you are feeling unhappy this evening, like your life is predictable and boring, perhaps you have been too rigid with yourself. Somewhere inside your adult exterior is a child who just wants to play and have a good time. As adults, we tend to anesthetize this playful self either through distraction (television, Internet, and, yes, work) or through various quick fixes (immoderate use of alcohol, drugs, and sex).

This evening, think about how your life might be different if you let your intuitive, playful self run free. Would you paint a picture? Walk barefoot through the grass? Before you go to sleep tonight, can you do one thing to let your inner child play? Can you list three things that you can do tomorrow to make yourself feel less confined?

# The World As It Is

*The truth does not change according to our*
*ability to stomach it emotionally.*

Flannery O'Connor, American author

You cannot *fix* the world; its patterns were set long before you were born. You cannot change other people; they follow their own interests and inclinations. Ultimately, you can only change your own thoughts and reactions. You can choose the kind of life that you want to live (to a degree) and how you *want* to be remembered. You can choose to speak up or be silent. You can control your actions but not their outcomes. We live in a world of radical contingency, but it is a world in which there is still space for freedom and choice. Choose wisely for yourself, and you will also become a model for others.

As you bring this day to a close, release thoughts of judgment and blame. Forgive others and yourself for not living up to your ideals. Allow yourself to accept the world as it is. Fix your inner landscape as the sole object of your desire for transformation. Allow intelligence, wisdom, and peace to fill your mind and heart. Let go of all traces of envy and malice. Within this space of meditation, become the ideal that you wish to see incarnated in the world.

# Peace Through Effort

*Never be in a hurry; do everything quietly and in a calm spirit.*
*Do not lose your inner peace for anything whatsoever,*
*even if your whole world seems upset.*

*Saint Francis de Sales, Bishop of Geneva*

We have a mistaken belief about peace, whether we are talking about peace in our individual lives or on the world stage, that it is a kind of absence, an absence of conflict or antagonism. And that gives us the false belief that peace is something passive, that it just drops down out of heaven. Peace is the hard-earned fruit of the labor for justice in human relations. We can bring about peace through our own efforts. On a personal level, this means cultivating peace through the process of meditation. On a national or international level, peace comes through holding the oppressor to account and by giving justice to the marginalized.

As you close your day, think of what you can do to achieve peace today. Perhaps you can say your personal mantra a few hundred times. Perhaps you can write a letter on behalf of a cause that means something to you. Perhaps you can reach out to someone on the margins of your society or social group. Feel a strong resolve within yourself to carry out your plans for peace.

# No More Delays

*There are some things you learn best in calm, and some in storm.*

Willa Cather, American author

Much effort in life goes wasted because we wait for the perfect conditions to act. We want plenty of free time, a big budget, support from others, and so forth before we will begin even a small project. Of course, the perfect timing, the perfect circumstances, never come, and we end up settling for less, delaying our plans indefinitely. It would be much better to work no matter what the circumstances. By working even when the chips are down, we can make ourselves more resilient, more patient. We become unstoppable.

This evening, you may find yourself full of regret that your heart's desire never seems to come. Think of one concrete step that you can take this evening to take you toward your goal. Can you work for five minutes on your book, paint or draw for ten minutes, go for a walk around the block? Do anything that might take you closer to your goals? Your mind feels restless because you hold back from living in the way that you think you should. Even the smallest effort will help to put your mind at ease and take you down the right path in life.

# Thinking, Feeling, and Acting

*Smile, breathe, and go slowly.*

Thich Nhat Hanh, Buddhist monk and peace activist

Thinking, feeling, and acting are linked together in a mutually reinforcing cycle. A positive action leads to positive feelings and positive thoughts. We can start at any link in the chain and move forward from there in the process of transformation. These three links of thinking, feeling, and acting also connect us to the other people in our lives. As we begin to make positive steps, we inspire others to do the same. This path of transformation is much preferable to the downward spiral of alienation and shame that dysfunctional communities inspire. So the choice is up to us, with each thought, each feeling, each action.

This evening, take a look at your own inner landscape. Take full responsibility for each thought, each feeling, each action. If you find yourself trapped in a dark mood that will not respond to your efforts to change it, perhaps a positive action will be more effective. You might try going for a walk or doing some yoga poses. If positive actions do not seem to work, try reading a book with an uplifting message. The most important thing to do is to keep trying to live peacefully, right up until you fall asleep.

# Action in Transition

*Nothing diminishes anxiety faster than action.*

Walter Anderson, painter, writer, and naturalist

All of us must act in this world, just by virtue of being born. Even sitting on our butts is a form of action. Doing nothing at all is still a kind of action, a choice with consequences. We cannot choose whether or not to act; we can only choose the manner of our action, the how and what and why of our doing. While we are, in a sense, condemned to action, we are also opened to possibility, since each moment brings the possibility of something new.

This evening you find yourself at the close of day. You're also at a transition point in your life, a season opening or closing. Know that no matter how much water has already passed under the bridge, you can still choose this evening who you will be. Take a few minutes at the close of this day to wonder about who you are and what you might become. Think about your highest ideals and what you would need to do to bring them into your life. What changes do you need to make to be the person you want to be? What would you need to add to your life to make that happen? What would you need to let go?

# You Don't Have to Be Super

*Take rest; a field that has rested gives a bountiful crop.*

*Ovid, Roman poet*

We put a lot of pressure on ourselves to think brilliant thoughts, enact strategic plans, and generally produce brilliant work. We forget that the mind is just a tool or instrument that only works so long as it has received constant care. If we overtax ourselves, if we do not get adequate food, rest, and exercise, the mind no longer works properly. Meditation, too, is one way of caring for the mind, letting it take a break from its labors. The mind emerges from the meditative state feeling refreshed, ready to tackle new challenges.

You may find yourself this evening wanting to be Superman or Superwoman. You might resent the time that it takes to cook a healthy dinner or get a good night's rest. You may wish that you could work robotically, day after day and night after night. Know that the time spent in rest is well spent, that you become a new person through sleep, which is also a portal into other worlds and new imaginings. Close your eyes tonight, confident in the belief that you will be remade while you dream.

# Fight That Sinking Feeling

*Calmness of mind is one of the beautiful jewels of wisdom. . . . The more tranquil a man becomes, the greater is his success, his influence, his power for good.*

James Allen, philosophical writer

The people who read my books probably think that I am naturally optimistic and cheerful. Truthfully, I'm more of an Eeyore than I am a Tigger. I have what used to be called a melancholic disposition. Fortunately, there is medicine to be found in words, to be found in mantra and prayer, to be found in long walks and good conversation. The difference between heaven and hell lies in the most subtle shift of perspective, and that is the benefit of mindfulness practice. Enlightenment is really just a different way of seeing the same old thing, letting go of a tired notion.

This evening, you may be inclined to take a dim view of life, and the world will certainly provide you with ample material to supply a lifetime of dark imaginings. But think for a moment that your sadness and depression harm only yourself and those you love. You may feel a sinking anchor in your heart, but keep fighting against it. Maybe you will always be a bit sad, but you can become more adept at managing your emotions. This will give you more room to maneuver and get to a better place.

# Healing over Heroism

*Heaven and earth and I are of the same root,*
*The ten-thousand things and I are of one substance.*

*Sengzhao, Chinese Buddhist philosopher*

We all go through seasons and even years in which it can be hard to see the beauty and the goodness in life. We may not even want to go on living. One thing that helps is to keep things very small and proximal, to have hope, not that the world will change or that all of our problems will go away, but just for some small thing that is captivating in some way. One needs only an interesting book to read or a friend to call on the phone or a single half-hearted interest. Everything else follows from there.

Oftentimes we think of spirituality in heroic terms, as astounding ascetic feats or writing mystical treatises or caring for lepers in the street. Sometimes the most spiritual thing that we can do is to care for this hurting self, to repair our wounds and go on living another day. Love of self, when understood properly, is the foundation for all other loves. Before you close your eyes this evening, release one cruel thought that you have had about yourself. Think of some small kindness that you can show yourself.

# Connecting Through Sorrow and Joy

*Be thou the rainbow in the storms of life. The evening beam that smiles the clouds away, and tints tomorrow with prophetic ray.*

Lord Byron, English poet

True wisdom remains always an aspiration, just out of reach. No matter how much we might try to remain open to the various contingencies of life, at some point a disaster will strike that makes the most stoic person break down. Nature will not be kind to inflexible plans: Murphy's Law remains in effect. If we are looking for the magic solution that will pull us out of the accidents of material existence, we will surely be disappointed. The best spirituality enables us to laugh at the worst of times and avoid smug superiority at the best of times. It takes us deeper into the human condition rather than rising above it.

This evening, as you bring your day to a close, take the time to savor everything that has occurred today, whether it is some small triumph or an event filled with sorrow. All of the negative and positive emotions are signs that you care about someone or something, that you are still alive, still an active participant in the drama of life. The next step is to see how your sorrow and joy are connected to someone else's sorrow and joy, to see how we are all part of the same mystery of being.

*Be* THOU *the* RAINBOW *in the* STORMS OF LIFE. THE EVENING BEAM *that* SMILES *the* CLOUDS AWAY, *and* TINTS TOMORROW *with* PROPHETIC RAY.

—Lord Byron, English poet

# Taking Responsibility for Emotional Reactions

*Nothing can bring you peace but yourself.*

Ralph Waldo Emerson, American essayist, lecturer, and poet

In our casual talk about our emotions, we often slip into a victim narrative: *He made me feel guilty, She made me mad.* It is okay to feel angry or guilty, but in truth, we actually can govern our internal states, which are just our own reactions to external events. We don't need to give control over our emotions to other people, especially not to people who may not have our best interests at heart. We have to learn to take a step back before reacting, to pause and breathe. Then we can better choose how to respond to what's happening. We can defuse the tense situation by breathing deeply and making detailed observations, both about what the other person is doing and what we are doing in that situation. A constructive plan of action can then be made that will provide a resolution with a minimum of self-pity.

As you look back over your actions today, did any situations arise that made you lose your cool? How might you have handled things differently? Are there any situations that arise on a routine basis in which you feel anxious, angry, or any other reactive emotion? Can you strategize about what you can do the next time this situation arises?

# Connection by Other Means

*Prayer is the key of the morning and the bolt of the evening.*

Mahatma Gandhi, lawyer and peace activist

With all of our technological distractions, we forget to return to the center of our being, to return awareness to the source. Our energies become scattered and diffused; life does not hold the same depth and satisfaction. Amusement is the enemy of contemplation, the killer of every impulse toward freedom, which comes only with self-discipline. In a society of consumers, having no entertainment is akin to death. In a society of contemplatives, having no entertainment is the beginning of tranquility. The spirit comes alive when distraction fades.

This evening, take a look at your media habits. Would you be willing to go without television and Internet for one week? For one day? For one hour? Do you get a twitchy feeling when you have to go without your cell phone for a few minutes? Are you capable of not checking your social media accounts? See if you can determine what effects technology has on your life, and make adjustments accordingly. Experiment with other means of connectivity, like seeing people in person, having a meal with loved ones, or writing a simple paper note.

# The Depths of
# Time and Nature

*This accidental / meeting of possibilities / calls itself I. / I ask:*
*what am I doing here? / And, at once, this I / becomes unreal.*

Dag Hammarskjöld, Swedish diplomat, economist, and author

This evening is the culmination of billions of years of cosmic time and myriad human and extra-human processes. The whole universe makes "you" possible, this moment possible. The universe courses through you, like electricity through a grid. You are made of the universe, and you belong to it. Nothing you can say or do could ever change this: We are all part and parcel of the cosmos, the origin and milieu of all of our actions.

This evening, open your awareness to the depths of time and nature that have come together to make this moment. You don't have to change anything or improve upon anything at this time. It is far more important to observe, to listen, to reflect. Look into yourself and inquire.

# Going Around a Blind Curve

*"Hope" is the thing with feathers / That perches in the soul /*
*And sings the tune without the words / And never stops—at all.*

*Emily Dickinson, American poet*

Living into the future is like going around a blind curve. We can make guesses and projections, but the future remains unknown. So we should never make the mistake of banking on outcomes that we calculate ahead of time. We have to make our peace with uncertainty, to be able to keep on living in the absence of complete information. Every act involves a certain amount of faith, because the element of the unknown cannot be eliminated from any undertaking.

This evening, you probably have in your head various projections about the future. You imagine what your day will look like tomorrow. You picture where your career and family will be five and ten years from now. You may even think about retirement and how you would like to spend your final years. Know that such plans are just partial and incomplete—possibly quite wrong—sketches for tomorrow. You need these plans in order to be able to function, but they do not exhaust the possibilities open to you. Make sure to leave room for what might be, for wonder and mystery.

# Dial It Back

*We are what we pretend to be,*
*so we must be careful about what we pretend to be.*

Kurt Vonnegut, American author

I often wonder if the thoughts that occupy our minds are just idle chatter or if they actually have import for how the world unfolds. Certainly some of those thoughts are telegraphed through space and time in the form of tweets, e-mails, articles, posts, chats, and books. Some of the thoughts sit in the waiting room of consciousness and their numbers are never called. Others are transmogrified into actions: guarded actions, hostile actions, kind actions, pathetic actions. These little mental creatures can take on a life of their own: They can sprout wings and fly away. It is best to be kind to them, to not rile them too much.

In the evening, especially, too much rumination causes indigestion and insomnia, paranoia and perplexity. Now take that from a confirmed ruminator, a fellow thought addict. Even if we don't succeed in eliminating thought, in achieving perfect calm we can still turn back the dial, making the thoughts less frantic, less irksome. See if you can turn back the dial right now. See if you can make the thoughts less insistent, more tranquil.

# An Expectant Frame of Mind

*Plans for the future are cut from a cloth not yet woven, stitched together with a thread not yet spun. The shuttle goes back and forth in the weaver's hands, and the rhythm goes on and on.*

Anonymous

Hinduism teaches a concept called *svadharma*, one's own personal duty, that is unique to each individual, yet bound together with one's family and one's role in society. This can be a liberating idea, because it means that you, specifically, have your own rightness, your own way of being in the world with responsibilities that are unique to you. This means that while there are moral precepts that do apply to everyone, you also have your unique mission to fulfill. No one can tell you exactly what that might be; you must find it yourself and actualize it yourself.

You have doubtless had moments of crystal clarity in your life, moments of epiphany when you suddenly knew what you had to do. Maybe you don't feel that way now; maybe everything seems confused and purposeless. Take a few minutes right now to breathe your mind and heart into a state of openness. Create the possibility for insight, for guidance, for clarity. Hold yourself in an expectant frame of mind, knowing that the answers will come to you.

# 108 Repetitions

*No man ever steps in the same river twice,*
*for it's not the same river and he's not the same man.*

Heraclitus, pre-Socratic Greek philosopher

A little bit of oil keeps a wrench from rusting. A little bit of lemon juice keeps apple slices from turning brown. A little bit of sunscreen keeps the skin from getting burned. A little bit of prayer and meditation keeps the dark thoughts at bay. Just a little effort, and then a little more, and a little more: so the road to liberation begins. One day all of those little efforts amount to something: an indomitable will, a tranquil frame of mind, and a joyful heart.

This evening say 108 repetitions of your favorite mantra or prayer. The number 108 is a sacred number in Hinduism having to do with the ratio of the diameter of the planets to their orbits and other mystical factors. A mala or rosary is strung with 108 beads plus one for the guru. If you don't have one, you could use a sacred word, like "peace" or "surrender." If your circumstances allow, light a lamp or candle and burn some incense during this time. If you are able, say another mala (set of 108 repetitions) or simply sit quietly for a few minutes. See if you detect a shift in your mental state after your meditation.

# The Place Beyond the Noise

*To do the useful thing, to say the courageous thing, to contemplate the
beautiful thing: that is enough for one man's life.*

*T.S. Eliot, American-born British author*

Two things are simultaneously true: that realizing God is the most simple
thing in the world, and that realizing God takes Herculean effort. If you
are a spiritual seeker, you know what I am saying. The experience of transcendence favors the childlike, beginner's mind. Once we begin to feel like
experts, the shine goes away very quickly; the lightning bolts don't come.
So we have to go back to a sense of wonder and awe, to forget everything
we already know and start from scratch.

This evening, as you sit and watch your thoughts, see if the expert voice,
the know-it-all voice arises. It may try to give you helpful suggestions or
provide running commentary. You may not be able to turn it off, but pretend like this voice is just meaningless background noise, like static on a ra-
dio. Go into that space of not-knowing and push farther into it. Eventually,
something more subtle and beautiful will emerge from that place beyond
the noise.

# Redirecting Anger, Resentment, and Jealousy

*Entering the forest he moves not the grass;*
*Entering the water he makes not a ripple.*

Zenrin Kushu, *a collection of writings used in the Rinzai school of Zen*

The value of *ahimsa* (nonharming) goes beyond refraining from killing living things. It also extends into our thoughts and words. It means not harboring any ill-will or blame toward ourselves or others. Striving for *ahimsa* gradually realigns our attitudes and assumptions. It is like the cool stream that gradually wears away the rough edges of stones and makes them as smooth as glass. We don't even really know or understand our own thought processes until we adopt the value of *ahimsa*. It is the means by which we come to see our own vengefulness and pettiness.

Watch your thoughts this evening: Do you see traces of anger, of resentment, of jealousy? See if you can redirect these feelings toward goodwill and love. Think of the object of your negative feelings as your dearest one: Treasure that person or object of anger as more valuable than life itself. See yourself in the face of the other and realize that peace only comes through acceptance.

# Night Mantras

*I took a deep breath and listened to the old brag of my heart.*
*I am. I am. I am.*

*Sylvia Plath, American author*

Sri Sai Baba of Shirdi, an Indian saint, is said to have slept at night on a narrow plank of wood, which also supported burning lamps. Similarly, the holy man Baba Lokenath kept a plank of wood next to him and slept while leaning against it. These holy men weren't torturing themselves with these unconventional sleeping arrangements: They just saw the value in remaining ever watchful and vigilant. They kept the nighttime, yes, as a time of rest, but also as a summons to contemplation.

Maybe tonight or some night this week you won't sleep very well. Rather than get upset about it, take some time do meditation or to read some philosophy or scripture. Don't go straight for the sleeping pills or television: Take some time for the life of the spirit. When you begin to feel tired again, go back to bed. Then you can have another small sleep and awake feeling more connected to the divine.

# Accepting the Body

*If your spine is inflexibly stiff at 30, you are old.*
*If it is completely flexible at 60, you are young.*

*Joseph Pilates, creator of the Pilates method of physical fitness*

The human body is a complex of interconnected systems, comprised of myriad biological processes, but it is still a material thing. It is certainly a marvel of design/creation, but it is still physical in nature, susceptible to decay, malfunction, and disease. Through normal processes of entropy, it gradually loses functioning until its eventual death. None of this means we should hate the body or abuse it: The body is a quite serviceable vehicle that sees us through good and bad times.

As you enter into your time and space of contemplation, take a mental scan of your body. Look for places of pain and tension. Breathe deeply into those uncomfortable places and observe them closely. Send wishes for relief and healing to those troubled spots. Look also for places of emotional pain that are located in the body: maybe body parts that you feel are ugly or are related to past trauma. Send feelings of acceptance and reintegration into these neglected parts of the body. Make peace with your body and be kind to it at the end of this day.

# Awareness of the
# Three Fields of Breath

*Learning to let go should be learned before learning to get.*
*Life should be touched, not strangled. You've got to relax, let it*
*happen at times, and at others move forward with it.*

Ray Bradbury, American author

This evening, you may find yourself rehashing the events of the day. Maybe you feel you have worked too hard, like you haven't gotten any fun or relaxation out of this day. Or maybe you feel you haven't worked hard enough, and you are berating yourself for being lazy or neglectful. Notice the "damned if you do, damned if you don't" quality of either narrative that you tell yourself. Give yourself permission to be satisfied with what you have done and what you have left undone. Tomorrow will be another chance to begin anew.

Take some deep inhalations, noticing the three areas of abdomen, side ribs, and upper chest. Try to breathe into each of these areas in isolation, and then fill all three with the inhaled breath. Think not only about inhaling air but about inhaling *prana*, the cosmic energy. Picture this energy moving up the spinal column, from the base of the spine to the top of your head and beyond. Picture a white light sending peace and healing to your mind and body. Let it purify your spirit of any feelings of regret or self-deprecation.

# Observing and Releasing the Emotions

*Very little is needed to make a happy life;*
*it is all within yourself in your way of thinking.*

Marcus Aurelius Antoninus, Stoic philosopher and Roman emperor

A mighty bull can be led with one pinky finger through the ring in its nose. A giant battleship can be steered with a wheel the size of a hubcap. A skilled martial artist can body slam a person many times bigger and stronger with a flick of the wrist. In the same way, our emotions, though very subtle, can get the better of our wits and govern our actions. This evening, are your emotions ruling you, or are you ruling your emotions? If you wanted to control them, could you?

Take a look at your emotional state at the close of the day. Notice whatever you feel, in a completely nonjudgmental way. Is it rage, frustration, joy, boredom, sadness, fear, lust? Attend as much as possible to the emotion, noticing its contours, its exact feeling. Once you have a good fix on it, realize also that this state is temporary: It has arisen, and it will fade again. Set this feeling adrift on the ocean of consciousness, and do not cling to it. Move into the observer position, and watch.

# Increasing the Quality of Your Interactions

*Friendship is the shadow of the evening,*
*which increases with the setting sun of life.*

*Jean de La Fontaine, French fabulist and poet*

Take a look at the connections with people that you have made today. Did you shut yourself away like a hermit, or were you the life of the party? Did you keep silent, or did you chatter away? Now notice the *quality* of what you said, did, and thought today. See your inner intentions magnified a hundred, a thousand, a hundred thousand times as the social connections ripple outward, from yourself to your intimates to your acquaintances to the world. So many philosophers and spiritual teachers have emphasized the importance of love, because everything we think, say, or do gets multiplied many times over. This is simply due to our nature as social animals.

Maybe you struggle with some sort of social awkwardness, or perhaps you go the opposite direction, into an excess of garrulousness. Know that, in any case, whether introverted or extroverted, your style of interaction can be a force for good in the world. Picture your thoughts, words, and actions as infused with care and concern for others. Resolve right now to say nothing unkind or injurious. Do not even think negative things about other people, and have this same attitude toward yourself as well.

# Dwelling in the Inner Darkness

*You cannot believe in God until you believe in yourself.*

Swami Vivekananda, Hindu monk

The turtle carries its home with it on its back. It can simply withdraw its arms, legs, and head into the safety of its shell whenever some threat looms. Its powerful armor will protect it from the fox and the alligator. Our human skins don't protect us much, but we do have an armor that protects us from the passions, the out-of-control emotions, the swamp of desires that infect our minds. That armor is called *pratyahara*, the withdrawal of the senses. When we shut our eyes in meditation and the curtain goes down, the darkness becomes a protective shell. Then we can go on into deeper concentration, and, if we are very persistent, union with the absolute.

Take the time now to close your eyes and breathe deeply. Explore the inner darkness for a few minutes. You may see some shimmering lights, and you may be able to hear the blood rushing in your ears. Concentrate on the spinal column, and then gradually bring your attention to the space between the eyes. Focus your attention in this space, and allow thought to dissolve. Remain here for as long as you can. If your mind wanders, you can always gently draw your attention back to this point.

# Feeling Just
# a Little Better

*Yes: I am a dreamer. For a dreamer is one who can only
find his way by moonlight, and his punishment is that he
sees the dawn before the rest of the world.*

Oscar Wilde, Irish author

Some emotions are fleeting: here for five minutes and then gone. I spill coffee on my shirt, I feel stupid, I change shirts. Then I forget about it. But some emotions are so deep-seated that they become a semipermanent backdrop to life. A few lucky souls are permanently lighthearted, but many of us suffer with depression and anxiety. Therapy and medication may help, but not as much as you might think. The good thing about these darker emotions is that they need not be defeated once and for all. We only need to fight them on *this day*, to find the resolve necessary to keep going.

This evening, you might be struggling with dark thoughts. Maybe you feel like you have wasted your life, or like no one cares about you. Maybe tomorrow looks bleak as well. For starters, detach from the flow of negative thoughts; stop adding one negative thought onto the previous. Then think of one small, positive thing. Take anything, past or present, that means something to you—your grandmother's smile, your

# YES: I AM A DREAMER.

*For* a dreamer is one who can only find his way by moonlight, and his punishment is that he sees the dawn before the rest of the world.

—Oscar Wilde, Irish author

favorite sweatshirt, a place you went on vacation—and just stick with that thought for a while. Make it as vivid as possible. If it should fade or turn into wistfulness or longing, switch to another good thought. Keep doing that until you feel better. It doesn't have to be *all the way better*— just a *little* better.

# Reboot the Mind

*Why do our mental processes so often seem to us to flow in "streams of consciousness"? Perhaps because, in order to keep control, we have to simplify how we represent what's happening. Then, when that complicated mental scene is "straightened out," it seems as though a single pipeline of ideas were flowing through the mind.*

Marvin Minsky, pioneer of computer science and artificial intelligence

If you try to run too many tasks on your computer or smartphone, it will perform poorly and probably crash. This is especially true when the connection is poor or the memory is nearly full. To make it run better, you have to close all of the apps or windows and restart the system. Usually this does the trick. In the same way, our minds function better when we are not trying to do too many things at one time, when our mental systems are not overtaxed. Meditation is a way of resetting our mental systems so that they run better. We all tend to overestimate our ability to multitask, and we overestimate the bandwidth of our mental systems.

When you sit down to meditate this evening, you may find that a dozen excuses instantly present themselves. Don't allow yourself to be dissuaded this evening. Sit down quietly, and allow all of your mental programs to close. Let go of your to-do list, let go of memory, let go of sensory processing. Allow your system to shut down, knowing that it will revive in a more optimal state.

# Empathy and Sympathy
# As the Default Condition

*A liberation movement demands an expansion of our moral horizons. . . . Practices that were previously regarded as natural and inevitable come to be seen as the result of an unjustifiable prejudice. . . . If we wish to avoid being numbered amongst the oppressors, we must be prepared to rethink even our most fundamental attitudes.*

*Peter Singer, Australian ethicist*

Empathy or sympathy are not the exceptions, but the rule of human emotional life. As social animals, we are wired for connection with one another. Indeed, consciousness is nothing but a series of intricate connections between centers of processing. Because we are built for the social life, the emotional states of those around us will inevitably creep into our own minds as well. This is why professional sports team and even rock bands hire psychologists to attend to the emotional state of the players. Each mind is a dense web of interconnections that is, in turn, connected to the environment and to other minds.

This evening, see if your mental state has been affected by those around you. Have you internalized the frustration, sadness, or rage of those around you? If so—good—you belong to the human race! At the same time, you should take the time to process these emotions. Look at each one of them in turn, and then release them into the flux, the endless stream of consciousness that runs before your mind's eye. Take the stance of the observer. Sit still and watch the thoughts and emotions as they come and go. After a long while, some plans of engagement may emerge.

# Shiva-Shakti Meditation

*He who firmly believes that God alone is the Doer and he himself [sic]
a mere instrument is a jīvanmukta, a free soul though living in a body.*

*Sri Ramakrishna, Hindu saint*

At the center of Indian philosophy is the Shiva-Shakti relationship. Shiva is consciousness, the passive partner, the masculine force. Shakti is nature, the active partner, the feminine force. The goddess is often depicted with her foot on the god Shiva's chest. This symbolizes his complete surrender before her, his complete absorption in nature. He has let go of all thought and allowed himself to worship Her with every fiber of His Being. This intertwining Shiva-Shakti relationship is the heart of reality, and it can be found in everything, from subatomic particles to the whirl of the galaxies.

The divine Shakti energy is the force behind all existence, and yet it is difficult to perceive. This evening, as you sit in meditation, allow yourself to become completely still. Learn from Lord Shiva as he meditates on his beloved. Become as still as a statue, as still as a corpse. When thoughts arise, see these, too, as part of Her nature. Worship everything that occurs before your consciousness as an aspect of the divine nature. Hold this frame of mind for as long as you can.

# Honor Your Body

*Meditation produces a reduced perception of pain overall,
not just during or around the time of the meditation.*

*Stephanie Burke, CEO and cofounder of Spine-health*

When something goes wrong with your body, like a chronic illness or an injury, it can suddenly feel like you have been dealt an unfair hand. The negative state of the body drives a wedge between your consciousness and the plans and projects that you had intended to accomplish. It feels like material nature is conspiring against you, like your own body doesn't belong to you. These unfortunate circumstances can become the occasion for practicing dispassion and detachment.

This evening, as you contemplate your body, you may see parts of it that cause you pain, that you do not like, that simply don't work properly. Work on practicing acceptance toward those flawed parts of the body that you do not like. Love the body, even though it betrays you. Be kind to it even if it lets you down. Practice nonviolence in thought, word, and deed toward this fragile instrument that carries you through life. While the body has not been invincible, it has been a good and faithful servant to you. Take the time to honor it now.

# Give Thanks for Gravity

*What we need is here.*

Wendell Berry, poet

Astronauts in orbit have health problems associated with the lack of gravity. They often have headaches and can even develop poor vision, perhaps having to do with the movement of fluids toward the head that would have normally been held lower down in the body by gravity. Sleep, too, presents a problem, as the astronauts must tether themselves in place to sleep. Imagine having to go to sleep without "down"! It would be quite an adjustment, but then I hear the view is great, too!

This evening, whether you are seated for meditation or lying down, feel the tug of gravity on your body, rooting you to the earth, your home. Feel that sense of intimacy with the planet, your home. Feel that reassuring tug downward. Whatever else might have changed today, no matter how much stress you might have in your life, some things remain the same, dependable. Release any tension that you might be holding, and give thanks for the earth, your home.

# Let Go of the Day

*There is a time for many words, and there is a time for sleep.*

Homer, The Odyssey

When you have a lot happening at work, whether it's a big deadline for a project, the interruptions of a troublesome coworker, or planning for a conference or trip, the tendency can just be to work nonstop until everything is done. The trouble is that hidden inefficiencies creep into your work. You may not notice that you are spending two hours prepping a presentation that should have taken twenty minutes. Your mind becomes clouded due to the lack of rest, and you may even find yourself getting physically ill.

As you come to the end of your day, you may find it hard to let go of the workday and settle into an evening of rest and contemplation. Notice the flow of thoughts going through your head as you make this transition. You may be guilt-tripping yourself for not working longer hours; you may be thinking of the stack of papers on your desk or in your work bag. Breathe deeply and let go of all of the pressing tasks that wait for you. All of your work will still be there tomorrow. After rest and meditation, you will be able to work both better and smarter.

# Bad Religion
# and Good Religion

*Every new gleam of light should be welcomed with joy.*
*Every hint should be followed out with eagerness.*
*Every whisper of the divine voice in the soul should be heard.*

William Ellery Channing, Unitarian minister

With all due respect to my atheist friends, if all of the religions of the world were to disappear tomorrow, we would still have war, poverty, inequality, greed, anger, ignorance, and all manner of human badness (we wouldn't be able to use the word "evil," with its religious connotations). Why would we still have the bad things in the world? Religion never exists by itself, but is always entangled with economics, politics, and, well, you know—*history*. We should stop the rather simplistic discussions of faith versus atheism and science versus religion and start talking about what makes for a good religion, which is the same thing as asking about *goodness in general* or how to be a good human being.

This evening, take a look at your own religious beliefs. Do they make you feel superior to other people, or do they help you to serve other people? Do your beliefs pull you into greater alignment with reality, or do your beliefs pull you away from reality? Do your beliefs help you to fulfill your duties in the world, or do they help you to escape from your duty? Are you after some sort of spiritual high, or are you after a complete integration of your personhood? Questions like these, when applied repeatedly and relentlessly, can help free us from destructive religion and bring us closer to truth.

# Sending Love to Your Connections

*Let us be grateful to the people who make us happy;*
*they are the charming gardeners who make our souls blossom.*

Marcel Proust, French novelist

Oftentimes, when we think of having a social life, we think of people who go to cocktail parties and gallery openings, people who have social calendars, who really have to check to see if they are doing anything before making plans. But having a social life could be much simpler: having a favorite table or a favorite server at the local diner, chatting with your spouse or a coworker, texting your mom or your sibling. So you don't have to have a sort of Hollywood social life; a few connections will do. Just try to make them as loving and complete as possible.

This evening, think of all of the people in your life, one at a time, as many as possible. As each person comes to mind, send them feelings of love and affection. Try not to think of any disagreements that you may have had in the past. Just send that person goodwill in the present. You may feel like calling some of them on the phone. If you do, that's fine, but don't make this a stressful exercise. Just reflect for a few minutes on the many people who have meant something to you over the years.

# The New, the Old, and the Very Old

*We cannot understand nature, other beings and ourselves, by going outside to any conceivable being. The growth of knowledge must be within the perceiver, the thinker himself. . . . But the thinker is the Self—the only Self, so far as he is concerned. . . . As action proceeds from that basis, the greater the powers which flow from that spiritual quality, the greater the increase of knowledge.*

Robert Crosbie, theosophist

Most Asian philosophies have an entirely different concept of time than in the West. Time is viewed as cyclical, not linear. If there is a concept of soul, it's that each one of our souls can neither be created nor destroyed. We all go through hundreds or thousands of lifetimes on our way to perfection. The world is viewed as an appearance, an illusion, called *maya*. This transitory world does not really exist, but it is an important school for the soul's development, a series of lessons that help us to move to a higher state. We keep repeating the same lessons until we have passed them, by not reacting violently or passionately.

This evening, at least as a thought exercise, picture your own soul as completely eternal. Picture yourself taking on many bodies, many lives, and then shedding them. What do you need to do in order to live more peacefully? What lessons in your life keep getting under your skin? What situations repeatedly make you lose your cool? Chances are, the things that bother you the most are exactly those places where you need to act constructively, but in a detached manner.

# Keep Exploring

*Mankind is slowly accomplishing its own suicide.*
*A self-strangulation is being effected through a*
*suppression of all individuality, in the spiritual sense,*
*and all that made it human. It continues to withhold the*
*spiritual atmosphere from its lungs, so to speak. . . .*
*The result is inner lethargy, chaos, and the disintegration*
*of all that formerly was held to be ideal and sacred.*

Israel Regardie, occultist

As a young person living in northeast Georgia, in the foothills of the Appalachian Mountains, my friends and I would spend whole days wandering around in the woods on Tower Mountain. Usually we would stick to the trails, but on occasion we would wander off through thickets of rhododendron and mountain laurel. Sometimes we found waterfalls not marked on the official signage. These ancient rocks, slick with algae, became sites for endless hours of climbing and sliding. We were so fortunate to be turned loose in the woods, to be able to entertain ourselves in the outdoors.

Our adult lives are so regimented with work and chores, so squeezed by responsibility, that we have to work at playing. Exploration no longer comes naturally in adult life; we have to seek it out. But those hidden waterfalls are available to those who look for them. We can find new wild places, unexplored places, in the terrain of nature or the inner landscape of the heart. We can explore using a map and compass or a pen and paper. The important thing is to keep wondering and keep asking questions. This evening, see if you can think of some unexplored places that you can visit, either in person or through inner investigation.

# Will Healing and Rest Into Your Body

*Awake, my dear. Be kind to your sleeping heart.*
*Take it out into the vast fields of Light, and let it breathe.*

Hafiz, Sufi poet

Our bodies have a way of storing, in physical form, the memories of past repetitive actions: The dancer's feet gnarl with broken bones, the football player's back ever aches, the writer's wrists whine angrily. We fit our bodies to our occupations and avocations; we take the physical form of our intangible avatars. We fit our members to the screen, to the keyboard, to the desk, to the bedside, to the office, to the factory. This mortal frame becomes our composition, intentionally or not. We may not be our bodies, but our bodies do receive the imprints of our thoughts and actions.

This evening, take a scan of your body from head to toe. Notice any pain or tension, and then explore it more deeply. If you notice pain in your shoulder, for example, is it a sharp, tight pain, or a dull ache? Is it the weariness of an honest day's work or a sign of some injury? You need not go into a long monologue; just take note of the pain. Then breathe deeply into the painful space, willing healing and rest into your body. Repeat this exercise two or three times before you reach for the medicine bottle.

AWAKE, MY DEAR.
Be kind to your
sleeping heart.
Take it out into the vast
fields of Light,
and let it breathe.

—Hafiz, Sufi poet

# Don't Be an Obtainer

*We began pretending the world was not designed in an
interconnected way. We've come to pretend that each of our
"goods" somehow originates from money rather than from a
particular farm, field, forest hillside, or cranny in a local ecosystem.
Children now think that milk comes from cartons.*

Tyrone Cashman, philosopher

Modern advertising is designed to make us feel inadequate in some way. *Do I look fat in this outfit? Is my car cool enough? Does my kitchen smell lemony fresh?* Of course, on some level we all know that it's nonsense. But time and time again, the manipulation gets into our skulls. The messages hammer away at us through thousands of repetitions, as in Aldous Huxley's *Brave New World*. We all secretly care what everyone else thinks, all while putting on a show of not caring. This is often called ironic participation, but irony is a pretty thin disguise for basically conformist tendencies.

The mystic and the artist really have a lot in common in that they both want to challenge the status quo and highlight the vacuous nature of societal values. This evening, ask yourself how you would live differently if you were really free. Imagine your life unconstrained by consumerism, what one of my friends called the "obtainer" mentality. Ask your inner guide to reveal to you some small way in which you might break free from social expectations.

# Disconnect Once in a While

*Being connected to everything has disconnected us from ourselves and the preciousness of this present moment.*

L.M. Browning, Vagabonds and Sundries

Consumer societies conspire against the life of the spirit. We are meant to keep going, to never stop, to always stay busy. We must work so that we can consume so that we can work. The treadmill works its way into our psyches, so that we feel a great discomfort whenever our time is not filled with something. Our conversation time, too, gets eroded by constant technological distraction. Any criticism of emerging technologies is met with the simplistic response of, "What are you, a Luddite?"

This evening, see if you can go media-free. Try to go for a couple of hours without the Internet. Utterly neglect your Facebook feed and most visited websites. Read a book made out of paper. Have a cup of tea. Paint, write, or draw. Play an instrument. See how the world does not fall apart without your participation in social media. See how your thinking changes when you do not go straight to your cell phone or tablet.

# Kindness Toward All People

*Do not protect yourself by a fence, but rather by your friends.*

*Czech proverb*

"Innovation" has become the buzzword of our time, the golden calf of early twenty-first-century capitalism. And yet the new tech startups have not done anything to ease growing inequality, to improve healthcare or education, or, you know, do the things that actually matter. Where is the app that can prevent warfare? Where is the startup that solves the refugee crisis in Europe? The point here is that we still need dialogue, skill in relating to one another. We desperately need better politics, more trustworthy institutions, less focus on "disruption."

This evening, return your mind and heart to the notion of care. Cultivate an attitude of kindness to people from differing backgrounds, toward people in distant lands, toward those who are less privileged. Think of what you can do to make our world a better place, in whatever industry you work, in the place where you live and the communities to which you belong.

# What Do You Seek?

*The Lord is his true home,*
*His pilgrim's tuft of hair, his sacred thread;*
*For he has entered the unitive state.*

Paramahamsa Upanishad

Once, in a small village, a man went to a fruit and vegetable dealer every day to buy lemons. His wife liked to take lemon in her water in the cool of the evening. Only sometimes he would get into the village and forget why he went there and would return home empty-handed, much to the annoyance of his wife. So she wrote "lemon" on his hand and sent him back to the village. The other villagers came to know this man as "Lemon" and laughed at him. But there was a certain upside to this ribbing, since the man would, from that day forward, get free lemons from the vendor.

In the same way, the devotee who does *sadhana* (spiritual practices) for God sometimes forgets why he or she does them. And yet the devotee is known by what he or she seeks and not necessarily what is accomplished. The devotee takes the name of the chosen divinity and becomes a devotee of Kali, of Ganesh, of Buddha, of Jesus, etc., gaining the protection and counsel—or the madness—of the chosen divinity. What is it that you seek this evening? How might your seeking come to define you? What would you risk to become identified with your chosen ideal?

# Weakness As Strength

*The moon shines in my body, but my blind eyes cannot see it:*
*the moon is within me, and so is the sun. / The unstruck drum of*
*Eternity is sounded within me; but my deaf ears cannot hear it.*

*Kabir, poet saint*

Even after teaching college students for many years, I still have a bout of nervousness before I leave my office to go into the classroom. I prepare my notes, I do my breathing exercises, I meditate, but there it is. The butterflies—more like mutant zombie flies—have invaded my stomach once again. I hesitate behind my office door, even though I am late. But then I say to myself, "This is the edge that allows you to perform at your best. The only remedy is action." I go to class, I teach, and often I enjoy myself.

This evening, perhaps you have some weakness that you can use as a strength, some tic or fault of yours that won't go away. Maybe just behind that weakness or fault lies some magic. You just need to know what to do with it. Be mindful this evening of some little quirk that you wouldn't want others to know about. Can you take this deficit and turn it to your advantage?

# Taking the First Step

*The future belongs to those who believe in the beauty of their dreams.*

*Eleanor Roosevelt, American politician, diplomat, and activist*

As human beings, we are deeply irrational, a fact that most philosophers forget. We will destroy our very life-support systems, create machine replacements for ourselves, kill our neighbors for a dime, and do almost anything if someone says, "I dare you." This trait of being, to put it kindly, risk loving, is at once horribly destructive but also beautiful and inspiring. It is as though we have been given compensation for our weak, hairless bodies in the form of a highly volatile rocket fuel for the imagination. Whether or not we destroy ourselves in the process is yet to be determined, but it will still be one hell of a ride!

If someone gave you a blank check to fulfill your craziest dream, what would you do? Think about this dream of yours for a few minutes this evening. Give this dream more texture, depth, and exactitude. Now imagine if you had to fulfill this dream without any resources or extra time. Can you think of one single, solitary step that you could take to make it happen? Resolve to yourself tonight to make that one small step.

# A Small Space
# of Resistance

*And forget not that the earth delights to feel*
*your bare feet and the winds long to play with your hair.*

*Kahlil Gibran*, The Prophet

Meditation and mindfulness have been co-opted by corporate America as the next big way to produce perfect little drones to manufacture ever more useless widgets for purchase by those very same perfect little drones. In this paradigm, meditation and mindfulness are another means of performance enhancement, another way of squeezing more units of production out of the same dime. Let the corporate overlords take the language of meditation and mindfulness: If these are the new buzzwords, fine. Only let's preserve within ourselves a small space of resistance and nonconformity, in which we know for ourselves that we are tapping into something more primal and real than a management seminar will ever be able to deliver. Let us become more ourselves, more human and real, because we meditate. Let's get back our sparkle and laughter. Let's get back our childlike joy. Let us let go of fear and intimidation. They want us to work ever harder, but we'll sing instead.

Has your mind been colonized by the drive to work so that you can consume (so that you can work)? Is there some carrot dangling in front of your face, some stick poised to strike your hindquarters? What would you do in your life if you didn't *have* to do it, if you weren't being paid or punished? Allow joy to be your motivator. If you can't recall the feeling of genuine joy, can you imagine for a few minutes what it might be like?

# Night Rituals

*The sky grew darker, painted blue on blue, one stroke
at a time, into deeper and deeper shades of night.*

Haruki Murakami, Dance Dance Dance

The night hides. The night hides from the sun, to be sure, but it also hides our deeds from the light. This doesn't have to be something sinister. Did you ever make a blanket fort as a kid? Remember how fun it was to stack up chairs and cushions, make tunnels and tents? You could read a book inside, tell stories and secrets, and it was all so much better inside the fort. That's what the night is like for adults. At night, when the day's duties are done, you finally have space to explore. You can be your own self, and no one can judge you. You can summon your own muses, don your own costumes, consume your own entheogens. The rites and rituals, the incantations and mantras, are yours to say: only the crickets and the streetlights listen.

Tonight the urge will be strong, overpowering even, to crash at the first sign of darkness. But you have work to do, and not the work given to you by the boss. I mean the work of your own awakening, the lifting of the veil, congress with spirits. Use this time to empower yourself to live into the future that you have only dreamed for yourself. Open the door to the unknown a tiny crack, and then open it wide. Do not let yourself sleep until your heart is satisfied.

# You Are an Instrument of Nature

*You can get to the ends of the world on a lie, but you cannot return.*

Russian proverb

A CEO doesn't really run a corporation, nor does a president run a country or a mayor a town. The leadership in any organization depends on the people ranked *below* him or her on the imaginary hierarchy concocted by society. A leader, from one step *behind*, reports on the activities of those in his or her care. What we call leadership really amounts to a fancy title with some ability to summarize information—in sometimes accurate and sometimes deceptive ways. An organization is an organism with many cells. When those cells are healthy, things get done. The leader doesn't even really guide this process.

This evening, forget about all praise and all blame that might attach to you at work or at home. Whether you have a high-ranking title or not, you are just the instrument, the conduit through which the forces of nature flow. Set aside the ego and look at your life in the harsh light of detachment: What do you see there? When you look inside yourself, what do you see there? Do you not see processes within processes? A tangle of thoughts, intentions, plans, projections? You will not see a firm center in the middle of all this. You will not see a doer behind the deed. The tangle goes all the way down.

# No More Second-Guessing

*May the stars carry your sadness away, / May the flowers fill your heart with beauty, / May hope forever wipe away your tears, / And, above all, may silence make you strong.*

Chief Dan George, chief of the Tsleil-Waututh Nation

How much time do you spend running scenarios in your head, with thoughts like, *Perhaps I should have done this instead . . .* Or, *Maybe if I had chosen x instead of y . . . ?* Implicit in this kind of exercise is an imaginary comparison between the present state of affairs and some imagined *better* state of affairs. This sort of thought exercise posits an alternate reality and then invidiously compares the present reality to the, well, *fake* reality. You will almost never come out ahead in such mental exercises, so it is best to stop running the scenarios as soon as possible. Say a mantra or recite the Declaration of Independence. Most thoughts are better than the proverbial Monday morning quarterback exercise of examining the past.

This evening, you may find yourself second-guessing something you did today. You may be replaying some incident in your mind again and again. Try talking about the situation with a loved one. Do some sacred reading or silent meditation. Lift the situation up to your favorite saint or spirit guide. Do anything other than continuing to ruminate on what you imagine that you did wrong. Who knows, maybe in the light of the not-too-distant future, it will become clear that your actions were entirely correct.

# Part of Something Bigger

*The most difficult thing is the decision to act.*
*The rest is merely tenacity. The fears are paper tigers. You can do*
*anything you decide to do. You can act to change and control your*
*life; and the procedure, the process is its own reward.*

*Amelia Earhart, aviation pioneer and author*

We live in a time of massive change: in the regime of information processing, in social and political upheaval, in interference with planetary systems. Think of what Gutenberg did for the written word and compare that to the impact of the Internet. Look at the advent of the nation-state, international terrorism, and the prospect of nuclear annihilation. Look how humankind can now alter the earth's systems in drastic ways. In the midst of all of these changes and breakages, interconnections and hostilities, it makes sense that our collective institutions and our individual psyches would be sent reeling on a day-to-day basis. Meditation and mindfulness will not solve the world's problems, but they may help to create a context, a supportive framework, in which those solutions can emerge.

Tonight, your head may be aching from your emotional and intellectual labors this day. Maybe you worked for hours at something that you don't really care about, or, hopefully, you poured your energies into your deepest labor of love. Either way, know that the solution does not depend only on you. You are a part of something much bigger than your-self. See yourself as one passenger on the great ship of humanity, a ship that is kept afloat by nature itself. Concentrate this evening on your own small part, your own limited duty, the routine wonderfulness for which you were born.

# Restoring the Common Good

*Do your practice, and all is coming.*

Krishna Pattabhi Jois, founder, Ashtanga Yoga Institute, Mysore, India

Philosophers love to debate the merits of free will and determinism: whether we, as humans, have somehow risen above the dictates of nature to become agents of our own destiny, or whether we are basically constrained by nature or society to take exactly those actions which we find ourselves taking. Social conservatives tend to argue for personal choice and responsibility, while social liberals tend to emphasize the impact of societal programming. And, of course, the debate can never really be won in the way that it has been framed. It is better to ask, what do I gain by taking one side or the other? How do I let myself off the hook, both for my own shortcomings and in terms of caring for others?

Let us not use philosophical arguments to excuse personal failings. We all have a part to play in creating the sort of society in which we want ourselves and our children to live. This evening, think about how you can contribute to the common good, to the well-being of all. Allow your heart and mind to will the good of all, not just your family or your social class. Send a heartfelt prayer or intention for all beings to have what they need to survive and thrive. Imagine a society in which no one lacks for anything, and let go of the cynicism and selfishness that says this is simply impossible.

# Small Adjustments

*Out beyond ideas of wrongdoing / and rightdoing there
is a field. / I'll meet you there. / When the soul lies down
in that grass / the world is too full to talk about.*

Rumi, Persian poet

If the bolt of the lock is perfectly aligned with the slot in the door jamb, the key will turn smoothly, with almost no resistance. If the door has swollen from heat or shrunk from cold, if the hinges are crooked from overuse, the bolt will stubbornly resist going into place. A little maintenance is needed, a little realignment. The hinges might need to be reset. Maybe the lock even needs replacing. Maybe the key needs to be filed. Maybe the lock needs a little graphite. So many factors for the proper turning of a bolt in a lock! If the lock on the front door needs so much attention, how much more so with our minds, our lives!

You may be going through a rough patch now, feeling depressed, bored, or alienated. The tendency in such situations can be to blow everything up and start all over: the divorce, the midlife crisis, the drug habit, etc. This evening, after a *generous* time of silent contemplation, think about the small adjustments you could make to your life, to make yourself happier and more functional. Think also about what is going well, the little successes that could easily be repeated. Many small adjustments eliminate the need for a major crisis.

# Don't Look Around the Corner

*When I admire the wonders of a sunset or the beauty of the moon,
my soul expands in the worship of the creator.*

Mahatma Gandhi, lawyer and peace activist

When I was a kid, I used to walk along the railroad tracks in Forest City, North Carolina, with my brother, my sister, and my cousins. We would find railroad ties and spikes, old turtle shells, and weird rocks. We would walk for miles, and the tracks seemed to go on forever. You couldn't see past the curve behind or before, but you knew the rails kept going. Time is a lot like that: disappearing to a vanishing point out of reach. We only have this point on the tracks, not the fading lines beyond the horizon.

As the evening light silhouettes the tree limbs against the darkening sky and the day's chores are finished, allow your mind to sync with your surroundings. You have done enough work today. Bring your mind to bear on this moment, the only time that you really have. Stay with whatever is happening right around you. Do not escape into fantasy. Do not plot or plan. Simply be here with this place and time. Breathe deeply into this present: receive the gift of this hour.

When I admire
the wonders of a sunset
or the beauty of the moon,
my soul expands in
the worship of the creator.

—Mahatma Gandhi, lawyer and
peace activist

# The Mind of Nature

*Difficulties exist only that in overcoming them we may grow strong,
and only those who have suffered are able to save.*

Annie Besant, British theosophist

You are one small facet of the mind of nature, one iteration within a giant sorting mechanism that has been going for billions of years. But don't think that being small and insignificant means that the things you do don't matter, for in the grand cosmic sweep of time, you are also absolutely unique. The possibilities in your mind are exactly the thoughts that the mind of God (or nature, whichever you prefer) has deigned to explore at exactly this locus in the web. This cosmic mind is omniscient *in you* and omnipresent *through you*: You are the eyes, ears, and, yes, the mind of God. That doesn't have to be a power trip, because the leaves on a maple tree and the dirt on the sidewalk are equally a part of the mind of God.

This evening, think for a second of all of the possibilities that the universe is simultaneously exploring, on this and on other worlds. Think of the infinite reaches of space and time—of all of the nebulae, black holes, and galaxies—the immense unfathomable grandness of it all. And think also that you, for some reason, have been given a place in it. And, for a few minutes at least, think of yourself as the instrument, as the outcome, of this cosmic history. Allow yourself to become the transparent, agentless vessel of boundless nature (or boundless thought, which amounts to the same thing).

# Live Your Senses

*As I grew up, everything started getting grey and dull. I could still remember the amazing intensity of the world I'd lived in as a child, but I thought the dulling of perception was an inevitable consequence of age—just as the lens of the eye is bound gradually to dim. I didn't understand that clarity is in the mind.*

Keith Johnstone, pioneer of improvisational theater

My toddler daughter has a pair of pink rain boots that are her favorite shoes. The pink rain boots give her puddle-stomping power, which brings her utter glee. Does she care that she is getting covered in mud from head to toe? No, she does not. Does she care that the water is going over the edge of the boots and soaking her feet? No, she does not. She takes off her shirt and struts around bare-chested with her brothers. She loves the dirt, the puddles, the rain, and the sky. Maybe those pink boots really are magical. . . . If only we adults could have one-tenth of this joy and enthusiasm.

We look at things, glance at things, all the time. But do we really pay attention? Do we really live in our surroundings, or do we just exist in them? In order to clean the mirror of the mind, we must first renounce the senses. But we cannot renounce the senses if we have not ever really engaged them in the first place. This evening, practice living fully into the senses, and then you will be prepared to enter the interior silence. Notice how that time in dark, silent contemplation actually sharpens and heightens the vividness of perception.

# Choose Who
# You Want to Be

*When we say that man [sic] chooses his own self,*
*we mean that every one of us does likewise; but we also mean*
*that in making this choice he also chooses all men.*

Jean-Paul Sartre, French existentialist philosopher

Powerful feedback loops amplify the smallest thought, word, or gesture when they are telegraphed through time and space, through real and virtual networks—a hall of mirrors effect when we act in the smallest way, so that each person passes signals thousands of times over each day. This creates a field effect that lifts or depresses the mood of every person or entity belonging to the network. Because of the social nature of human beings and the interdependent nature of our evolution with other species, these networks are near infinite. With each interaction, we change the course of humanity and the future of the world.

This evening, you choose for yourself who you want to be. Your choice ripples outward to all of humanity and to extra-human nature as well. There is no opt-out clause for our involvement in the universe. Choose compassion, peace, and kindness for all beings. See goodwill rapidly enveloping all of humanity and nature as well. Realize your union with the whole.

# Sharing Your Knowledge

*To teach is to create a space in*
*which the community of truth is practiced.*

Parker J. Palmer, American author and educator

My friend, James Carl, taught me how to change the oil in my car when I was in college. It felt so different from my university studies to put the car up on ramps, remove the drain plug, and watch the old, cruddy oil slowly fill the drain pan. Here was something tangible I could do, with my own hands, to make this machine run better. I only saved maybe ten bucks by doing it myself, but it was worth the effort to learn something new and spend time with my friend. He even asked me to stay for dinner, and I met the whole family.

We are all teachers in one way or another; we all know something that others don't. We carry this knowledge in our minds, but we also pass it down in our families and our communities. We all have a treasure trove of stories and skills. This evening, what do you know that you have been reluctant to share? Do you have a hidden talent that needs to be released into the world? Think of one way that you can be less guarded about your gifts.

# Outside As Antidote

*The mountains are calling and I must go.*

John Muir, naturalist

These days, we spend so much time in the virtual world that we are in danger of becoming brains in vats. Our physical bodies atrophy, as do our social skills and life skills. The real and the virtual are not exactly opposites; they bleed into one another. But let's not forget the old ways of doing things, with a handshake and a smile. As we build new worlds, extending into cyberspace and outer space, let's remember our grandparents, who worked the soil with their own hands, who ran the mills and factories from whistle to whistle.

When you are feeling low on insight, when nothing makes sense—though your mind is racing—go outside. Go outside this evening, if only for a few minutes. You don't need much of an agenda, other than paying attention. Listen to the squirrel clucking in the pine, the drone of distant cars on the highway. Feel the cold or the humidity on your face. You will start to feel better within minutes: less confused, more alert, more focused. Spending time in nature is like a bath for the mind.

# Expansion of Human Potential

*In addition to the struggle against misery, injustice, and
exploitation, what we seek is the creation of a new man [sic].*

Gustavo Gutiérrez, Peruvian liberation theologian

For all of the criticism of religion by scientists and technologists, both forms of discourse aim at the unlocking of latent human potential. What appears, at a surface level, to be an antagonism between science and more traditional modes of thought is actually deeply symbiotic. Philosophy, ethics, and religion enjoin scientists to consider the broader good in their work, while scientists and technologists implore the (shall we say) metaphysically minded to reject preconceived limits to human advancement. The relationship between science and religion is like the double helix of a strand of DNA, spiraling upward through the contentious process of dialectic.

This evening, take some time to read about a new scientific discovery before doing your meditation. Make it something that you are barely able to understand, maybe a branch of math or physics. Consider the exercise of your intelligence to the utmost to be a form of spiritual practice. Then, as you sit in meditation, allow your understanding of what it means to be human to expand. Consider the ways in which biology, technology, and what we might call *the soul* all intertwine.

# Setting Aside Time for Illumination

*O adorable Lord [Agni], we kindle your light, bright and undiminishing, so that its blazes keep shining deep in our hearts. May you, O Lord, grant nourishment to those who adore you.*

Rig-Veda V.6:4–6

At some point in your journey of meditation and mindfulness, you will want to go beyond the beginning stages to deeper realization. Probably by now you have had some flashes of insight and inspiration. You have likely had surges of positive feelings. In order to go further—and here is the hard part—you must *send back* these gifts of the spirit. You have to reject them, hold onto your seat, and look for a more direct experience of ultimate reality. This can take hours or days, but everyone should, at least once, have the experience of going as far as internal inquiry can take them.

This evening, get out your calendar. Find one day in the next month that you can set aside for meditation. When the day arrives, block out all forms of entertainment and distraction. Allow yourself only mantra and meditation, and perhaps some light food and exercise. This one day of retreat will make a great difference in your practice, more so than many months of halfhearted, occasional exertion. Just keep in mind that you cannot fully control the experience: Illumination happens on its own timetable.

# A Time for Quiet Mourning

*Each species is a world in itself. It is a unique part of Nature.*

E.O. Wilson, entomologist, conservationist, and author

Nature has an intelligence of its own that finds the right way, the most efficient way, to secure the means of life. We have only just begun to understand the workings of various biochemical processes that supply us with new medicines and therapies. We are learning to encode information biologically, and the boundaries between the living and the nonliving have never been more uncertain. At the same time, the colossal hubris and stupidity of humankind now imperils the natural world as never before. Mass extinction, climate change, and warfare threaten the future of the vast storehouses of nature.

Many people deal with ecological crisis with a head-in-the-sand approach: They pretend like nothing is wrong, like civilization can just go on forever on its present trajectory. This evening, allow yourself a few minutes of quiet mourning for the species that humankind has killed and is currently driving toward extinction. Feel in yourself a growing resolve to fight for the earth and its creatures. Strive to eliminate the ignorant, arrogant attitude of human superiority over nature. Realize your own animality, and let that be a catalyst for change.

# The Way Not Yet Invented

*There are two ways of spreading light:*
*to be the candle or the mirror that reflects it.*

Edith Wharton, American author

The average hunter-gatherer could identify hundreds of species of plants, could navigate by the stars, could make a living with a few simple tools. By contrast, most consumers today struggle to identify perhaps a dozen plant species and can maybe locate a constellation or two, if they bother to try. Most people in wealthy consumer societies would die without automobiles and supermarkets. Our comfort comes at the cost of great ignorance about nature and great alienation from nature. Not to mention the incredible wastefulness and violence of our lives.

People of conscience long for a better way: for a stronger connection to the biome, for less destructive ways of life. The best minds of today are those who make a more sustainable future possible. This evening, allow yourself to welcome the possibility of a new way of being human, a way that does not require the massive death of ecosystems. Maybe this new way has not yet been invented, but keep a space open for it in your mind and heart. Be on the lookout for it, and work for its discovery.

# Practice Ahimsa

*Do not injure, abuse, oppress, enslave, insult, torment, torture, or kill any creature or living being.*

*Mahavira, the twenty-fourth Jain Tirthankara*

The religions and philosophies stemming from the Indian subcontinent—Hinduism, Jainism, and Buddhism—all place *ahimsa*, or nonharming, as a central value. Some people believe that *ahimsa* is a primarily negative value, since it is about, well, *not* doing something. But actually when this principle is allowed to inform everything, from logic to politics to agriculture to engineering, it transforms whatever it touches. *Ahimsa* is extremely creative and generative, if we could only allow it to gain more of a foothold as a working principle, even a *design* principle.

Ahimsa is a discipline, that is, something that requires work and continual practice. This evening, watch your thoughts for qualities of aggression, resentment, and anger. Continue to unspool the thread and see how these thoughts might lead to aggressive actions. Shed these negative tendencies through an internal release or surrender. Don't be discouraged if you don't succeed right away: Practicing *ahimsa* requires a complete revolution in consciousness. It takes a lifetime of practice, even with the best of intentions.

# Space Clearing

*Communication is life-alienating when it clouds our awareness that
we are each responsible for our own thoughts, feelings, and actions.*

Marshall B. Rosenberg, Nonviolent Communication

The most difficult thing of all is the control of our own thoughts and emotions. If we wrestle with them directly, this often just magnifies the problem. I am angry, so I think about the source of my anger, which then focuses the emotion, just as a magnifying glass intensifies the solar energy coming from the sun. One can redirect attention toward something entirely unrelated, one can practice mantra or silent meditation, one can physically relocate into a less stressful environment. These are ways of circumventing the disturbing emotion without magnifying it. A general on the battlefield has an array of techniques for attacking the enemy: Some rely on stealth; others are more direct. In the same way, we need many ways of confronting reactive thoughts and their accompanying emotional states.

This evening, take a look at one part of your home that causes you emotional distress. Paying very close attention to your mental and emotional space, clean and rearrange that space, being very careful not to arouse resentment or other negative reactions. Clear the space mindfully, keeping alert to any possible disturbances, internal or external. Continue until you have calm inside and order outside.

# On Idol Worship

*Namo mahadbhyo arbhakebyaścha vo namaḥ*
*We bow . . . to he who is the great and who is the small.*

Rudrāṣṭādhyāyī, *V.26, trans. Swami Satyananda*
*Saraswati and Swami Vittalananda Saraswati*

Religious ritual is largely maligned in Western culture, due to the influence of Protestantism. The story goes that practicing rituals amounts to a superstitious form of mental slavery, in which the primitive religious mind clings to fetish objects for magical control of the universe. But by eliminating the supposed idols of religious practice, Protestantism smuggled a legion of new idols in the backdoor, idols like capitalism, consumerism, scientism, and, yes, secularism (a kind of ultra-Protestantism). Everyone worships idols of one form or another; only the bold and free person can take conscious control of this process and deliberately steer the worship of idols to the incarnation of the ideals that they represent.

Have you ever been shamed into dropping some form of ritual worship? Have you hidden religious statuary or pictures because of fear of what others might think? Do you shy away from rituals because of beliefs inherited from childhood? This evening, unleash your inner heathen and concoct a ritual of your own, or try some ancient practice that you have always wanted to explore. Find a small space in your home where you can freely express your religious beliefs, including your religious aesthetic. If you consider yourself atheist, you probably still have heroes that you venerate in some way. Perhaps you could hang a picture of your favorite scientist or inventor.

# Enjoy Protection from the Divine Mother

*Do not anticipate trouble or worry about*
*what may never happen. Keep in the sunlight.*

Benjamin Franklin, Founding Father, United States

Indian philosophy teaches that the world as it appears to the untrained senses is *maya*, or illusion, the *leela*, or play, of the Goddess. Why does She choose to take the guise of the stranger, the forest, the flower? Why does She allow this turbulent mental life, this maelstrom of emotions? Is there really anything apart from Her? Well, we can't say why She chooses to appear in the ways that She does: It seems She likes masks and hide-and-go-seek. The true tantric teachings that come down to us through God-as-guru show us that we can peek behind the mask by worshipping *maya* as the face of the Goddess. If we can see duality as one of Her moments or movements, we can experience Her reality and come into union with Her.

This evening, you may have aspects of your life that seem decidedly less than divine. You are beset by worry; you have a thousand obstacles in your path. Your past will not go away. How do you defeat the demons? By communing with She who is the Divine Mother, the Empress of All. You don't have to destroy the demons: just take shelter at Her divine feet. She will protect you. Picture the goddess any way you like—as Durga, as Kali, as Lakshmi, as Quan Yin, as Mary—and sit at Her feet. She will melt away the worry and stress. Surrender to Her, and she will take care of everything for you, Her child.

# Back from the Brink

*You ask me why I stay up here / alone on the green mountain. /*
*I smile, but give no other answer— / and yet, my heart's at leisure.*

Li Bai, Chinese poet

One the one side: the maw, chaos, destruction, oblivion, nonexistence, the void. On the other side: love, caring, concern—these warm and fuzzy sentiments that people discount actually make things go; actually make consciousness itself go. Without some act of love, it is impossible to form a sense of self, and then a meaningful narrative of a life. When I say "narrative" I mean, at the most basic level, before and after, this happened and then this. I am here, the wall is over there. These basic structures of reality are mediated through caring; without caring, there is no mind. Even the most disturbed individual, the most manipulative, had to have nurturing at some stage of life to even have the will to live, to have a personality to express.

This evening, think of a time when you felt yourself teetering on the brink, perhaps during a suicidal episode or a traumatic event. What thoughts helped to bring you back from the precipice? By examining what keeps you alive, what gets you out of bed in the morning, you will find your purpose and meaning in life. Do what feeds you, what keeps you alive and at least somewhat joyful. By persisting in the things that make you feel alive, you will become strong and courageous.

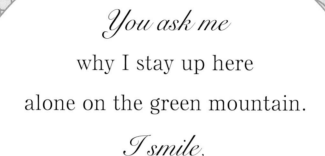

*You ask me*

why I stay up here

alone on the green mountain.

*I smile,*

but give no other answer—

and yet,

MY HEART'S AT LEISURE.

—Li Bai, Chinese poet

# Seek Balance

*Human perception organizes sense out of space and time.
If you change the ratios (as McLuhan would say), you change
the person. "Ratio" is the root word of "rational."*

*Paul D. Miller, aka DJ Spooky*

*La dah dah dah dee dah dah dah dah. Shoo bop sha wow wow. Baby, baby, baby.* Where would pop music be without basically nonsensical sounds? It just goes to show that music, like life, is not primarily about the proper ordering of concepts. That is a hard lesson for a philosopher to swallow, but what is lost in the form of logic is regained in the form of music. Living according to melody is much easier than living according to the dictates of reason. Reason—what an unattainable, undefinable, cruel ideal! But the strains of music lift the disillusioned idealist to a better place in the heart: What is lost in the world can be regained in the space of sound.

We spend so much time in the fruitless and untrue opposition between mind and heart. What if the two are not bitter enemies but lovers intertwined? This evening, make the journey into the heart center, and concentrate your attention here. Find and balance the masculine and feminine energies, the left and the right side of the body, the thinking and the feeling self. Gaze on this vital center, and feel the currents of vital energy making it blaze brightly with universal compassion. Hear the music of rushing blood commingle with the music of the spheres.

# Infinite Goodness and Infinite Possibility

*I am determined to be cheerful and happy in whatever situation I may find myself. For I have learned that the greater part of our misery or unhappiness is determined not by our circumstance but by our disposition.*

Martha Washington, first lady

It is very easy, the easiest thing of all, to come up with excuses for not doing the practice. *I didn't have enough time. I need more money. No one understands me.* These self-justifications might even be true, but they also don't lead anywhere. They are the dead ends of the spirit, stopping places for all dreams and visions. To accomplish something in spirituality *or any other aspect of life*, we need a new narrative. This new narrative says, *let me do what I can do today*, even for just ten minutes. Let me put my resources, even ten cents, toward this thing that I truly love and want to see born into the world. The universe can work with small efforts, but it cannot work with excuses.

This evening, breathe deeply into the diaphragm, the side ribs, and then the chest. See how a deeper breath naturally makes the carriage of your spine more upright. Breathe into the painful places; allow them to receive healing. Hold in your mind an idea of infinite goodness and infinite possibility. Allow yourself to believe in this infinite goodness and infinite possibility. Allow yourself to believe that it lives in you. Allow yourself to believe that it lives in your little projects and your crazy ideas. Feed this spark of possibility with your thinking, willing, and action.

# Drop the Veil

*Your material life, your desires for everything material and your natural tendency for yearning [for] material happiness—all these have been divinely designed to take you to a plane of higher evolution.*

*Baba Lokenath, Hindu saint*

The difference between the holy and the mundane rests on a change in attitude or perspective. If I think that nothing is sacred, then nothing is sacred. If I think that everything is quotidian and uninteresting, that will become true for me. The mind colors every sensation and experience with its own predisposition, such that we see the world filtered in a certain way. If we could drop all preconditioning, we would be overawed by the complexity of our surroundings, unable to process the exquisite beauty of everything. The veil stays put most of the time; otherwise, we would not be able to do anything or maintain sanity.

But the veil must also drop some of the time, or life becomes dull. Perhaps it will drop for you tonight. Perhaps you will see clearly, unguardedly. Do not simply look, but behold your surroundings. Do not simply hear, but listen deeply. Use your great power to will your mind into stillness. Exhort the many things to reveal their true nature to you. Demand to see table, chair and lamp, tree, grass, and shrub as they are, not as your conditioning has expected them to be. Persist. Go further than you have before. Push past all resistance, within or without.

# You Are More Free
# Than You Think

*Do what you can, with what you have, where you are.*

Theodore Roosevelt, twenty-sixth president of the United States

Most of the time our dissatisfaction comes from shortchanging ourselves. We give lots of effort to the things we don't really care about but little effort to the things we care about the most. Some would say that where we spend our time and money reflects our true values, but I don't believe that to be the case. We can live in such a way as to quash our dreams, push them so deep inside, but they don't really go away. The good news is that any moment we can get back to the things we care about, whether it is practicing meditation or playing a musical instrument or collecting postage stamps.

This evening, can you carve out a few minutes for the things you care about, for the activities that feed your soul? Are you having internal resistance to the idea that you deserve a few quiet minutes to yourself? If so, observe that feeling of guilt or whatever it is that is holding you back. Know that you deserve to be whole and well; you deserve to be centered and alive. Know that some of the pressures you feel have been magnified by your own internal dialogue. You are more free than you think, right now.

# Recognizing a Good Society

*The kingdom of God is within you.*

Luke 17:21

Contrary to popular opinion, the challenges of the twenty-first century are not primarily technical in nature but are the exact challenges that were at the forefront of the minds of ancient thinkers. We most desperately need to ask *how to build just societies, how to distribute resources fairly, how to live good lives in good societies.* Unless we can come to grips with basic questions of justice, all of the technological innovations in the world will be of no use. Without ethics, advanced technologies become just one more way for the wealthy and powerful to siphon resources toward themselves at the expense of marginalized people.

This evening, take a few minutes to contemplate the question of what a just society, what a good society, would look like. Jot down your ideas on a sheet of paper, and then ask what your role in such a society would be. Over the coming days and weeks, be on the lookout for anyone who might say that a just society is impractical or impossible. Such cynical denouncements often mask a fundamental disregard for the well-being of people and the planet.

# Interconnection and Change
# As Fundamental Reality

*When I roam the life cycle driven by strong hallucinations,*
*May the host of mild and fierce Lords lead me on the path*
*Of the light that conquers terrifying visions of hate and fear!*

The Tibetan Book of the Dead

One of the basic themes of Asian philosophy is the interrelated nature of liberation, that I can't secure my release from suffering at someone else's expense. We are all part of one web of humankind, which is in turn part of the web of nature, which is a never-ending cycle of destruction and new beginnings. Many Western thinkers, like Pythagoras and Socrates, also believed in reincarnation and cyclic existence. Whether or not you believe in reincarnation, it is profoundly sad that we have lost the notion of a common lot with other human beings and other species.

This evening, as you breathe deeply and concentrate on this present moment, see all of the processes that go into making your life possible. The food in your stomach came to you by means of supply chains extending, in many cases, around the world. You breathe in the air supplied to you by billions of years of evolutionary change. Realize interconnection and change as the fundamental reality; allow the dream of ego and duality to dissolve.

# Taking a Personal Vow

*"Love" is just the name we give to the desire for and pursuit of wholeness.*

*Plato,* The Symposium

Something attracted you to the practices of mindfulness and meditation: Was it the words of a teacher or mentor? Was it participating in a religious or ethical community? An article you, by chance, happened to read? Allow yourself to admit to the possibility of mindfulness as your life's mission. Perhaps you were *meant* (however you want to think about that word) to dedicate your life to the transformation and expansion of consciousness. Perhaps you were born to find a path to enlightenment (again, however you wish to interpret that word) for yourself, and, in turn, to teach others the way that you have found.

Many spiritual paths allow adherents to take a personal vow (*vrata*), either for a short period of time or for life, in order to facilitate the deepening of spiritual practice. Consider such a vow for yourself, right now. Perhaps you would like to switch to a vegetarian or vegan diet. Perhaps you can commit to studying a particular scripture or practice. Perhaps you can commit to a certain number of minutes or hours each day for meditation, or maybe you can rise an hour earlier each day. Make this vow something doable and something meaningful to you. Be cautious about broadcasting your intentions to others, although you might tell your spiritual teacher.

# Between Risk
# and Resignation

*Spiritual aspirants should rid themselves of all ego and
be free from malice towards others. They should try to
see the same Atma (Spirit) as inherent in all. They should
abstain from reviling others. . . . If you slander anyone, it is
tantamount to slandering God Him[Her]self.*

*Guru Charitra*

Each of us have contradictory urges and drives that make it very difficult to find peace and fulfillment. We want financial stability and physical safety, but we also crave adventure and excitement. Adventure and
excitement necessarily mean accepting a certain level of risk, or expo-
sure to a certain level of harm (i.e., the opposite of security and stability). So we find ourselves walking a fine line between boredom on the
one hand and recklessness on the other. Most people forever cycle between these two poles. This is not necessarily a problem, but it is useful
to just notice this dynamic and our place on the spectrum at any given
point in time.

This evening, do you find yourself in the doldrums, looking for excitement and stimulation? Or do you find yourself having taken a great
risk and perhaps regretting it? Can you find your own happy medium

between risk and resignation? Take a look at your life, as it is right now, and find ways in which you could take acceptable, productive risks. Look also for places where you have unnecessary, harmful risk. Make peace with the level of risk that seems right for you, in all aspects of life.

# Speak Kindly to Yourself

*Children often possess gifts which they lose as they grow up. With the years we seem to enter into a prison of conventions and opinions, concealments and unquestioned acceptance, and there we lose the candor of childhood. The child still reacts spontaneously to the spontaneity of life.*

Karl Jaspers, German philosopher

Living a compassionate life does not only apply to caring for other people. It also means self-compassion. True, the Hindu and Buddhist traditions view the self, understood as the personality or ego, to be an illusion (the differences between the traditions have sometimes been overstated), but one can still cause suffering through mental violence. It is as though we make a piñata out of the elements of consciousness and then proceed to beat that piñata with the stick of criticism. One can defuse this dynamic by seeing through the ego (dismantling the "piñata") or refraining from inward criticism (putting down the "stick").

This evening, watch the way that you talk to yourself. Speak kindly to yourself and utter not a single harsh word, not even in your head. If you must talk to yourself inwardly, say only kind, encouraging things, as though you wanted to be a good friend or coach to yourself. Say things like, "You really did a great job on that presentation today," or "You are such a good and caring person." This might feel strange, but continue with the practice anyway. See if you do not experience a better mood over time.

# The Small Sounds of Nature

*Nothing else can be said about God as God which is not symbolic.*

*Paul Tillich, theologian*

I happen to live right next to the Savannah River and the Augusta Canal, which makes for great long walks and nature watching. Anhingas, egrets, and herons walk on their stilt-like legs and fish in the shallows. Small alligators stealthily ply the water. Turtles pile on top of one another on every jutting log. And don't forget the people kayaking, biking, walking, and running. It is easier to breathe out here, easier to let go of all of the worries of the day, easier to just be.

This evening, pay attention to the small sounds of nature all around you. Open your eyes and ears. Increase your sensitivity to your surroundings—urban, suburban, or rural. Think about all of those little creatures, making a living by doing their thing. Allow a little bit of that wildness to enter your own consciousness; become, for a while, another animal in nature. See how the other creatures take no more than they need, make themselves at home wherever they are, and blend seamlessly into their surroundings.

# To Observe Is to Change

*The fact that you were aware of your mental wanderings or of your inner turmoil or of your inability to be still shows that you have some small degree of silence within you, at least a sufficient amount of silence to be aware of all of this.*

*Anthony de Mello, Jesuit priest*

With frequent practice, meditation becomes a powerful way to regulate emotion. A master meditator does not become uncaring or stoic necessarily, but she does have a greater degree of freedom to select which feelings will be entertained and under what conditions. There is no harm in feeling sad when a dear friend has passed or joyful when some important milestone has been passed. The emotions are only a problem when they are disproportionate to the occasion or when they run the show. At this point, they have to be brought back into line, almost exclusively through careful, deliberate attention.

It might seem strange to say that simply by observing the emotions closely one can change them. Try it for yourself this evening. Take a look at your feelings and see if you can break them down into their component parts. Maybe you will be able to see persistent thought patterns associated with a particular feeling or physical sensations associated with, say, sadness or anger. Simply pay close attention to the feeling, and see if that observation does not change what is being observed.

# Exploring the
# Boundaries of Pain

*The compass and the square bring to perfection the square and
the circle. The sage brings to perfection human relations.*

Mencius, Chinese philosopher

As we get older, mobility decreases, and one form of pain or another becomes a daily reality. People in first-world nations, especially the United States, have developed a strong propensity toward medicating pain to make it go away. This has terrible consequences in the form of the current opioid epidemic. The trouble with medicating pain is that pain is part of the healing process and part of life itself. Mindfulness practices teach something quite the opposite: to observe pain closely and live with it. This does not have to be masochistic. It is simply to accept the given reality and adapt to it.

If you are having some physical or emotional pain this evening, press against the boundaries of that pain. Do not be reckless; just try to keep the pain from having the final say. Go about your routine in spite of the pain. Resist the temptation to go straight for the bottle of pills. See if you can safely expand, ever so slightly, your range of motion. Expand your mental and emotional space as well by working against the tendency to allow pain to dictate the terms of your life.

# Hospitality As a Duty

*At the impulsion of power, we praise the mother Earth, Aditi (indivisible) by name. On this Earth, where all this life has been accommodated, may the creator God provide shelter to us.*

Yajur Veda 18.35.30

Hospitality to the stranger is regarded as a central ethical duty in most of the world's religions, and yet that tenet of belief is so easily set aside. At the time of this writing, Europe has developed a fortress mentality to prevent migrants from war zones from entering the continent. In America, appalling racism and xenophobia is directed at migrants from Central and South America. Mindfulness helps restore our wits, to see people as people and nationality as fiction. If we cannot welcome others, we cannot come home to ourselves either.

This evening, search your consciousness for traces of resentment or cruelty toward others who may not belong to your ethnic group or social class. As you breathe deeply into your heart center, eradicate all traces of animosity that you find there. Resolve to be more welcoming and open to all people. Resolve to defend those less fortunate than you. Resolve to speak on behalf of justice whenever the opportunity presents itself.

# Problems As
# Teachers in Disguise

*I believe that there was a day not long ago when humans were
more in touch with their mental abilities, and were maybe
not always capable of literal communication with animals,
but at least capable of conveying intense feelings of fear and
respect. . . . A door is closing, one that in the past led to a world
where animals and humans lived harmoniously.*

*Rod Coronado, activist*

As young people, we have our heads filled with all sorts of harmful illusions. We think that we will automatically find fulfilling and highly paid careers in the field of our choice. We think that romantic love will be enough to solve all of the problems we face. We think that life will be like a television sitcom, with a cast of witty and helpful characters, on call at a moment's notice to help us with the amusing crisis of the day. In real life, the solutions do not come so easily; the episode does not end with everything neatly resolved. The problems keep coming, and they often do not go away, even with years or decades of work. But we can still laugh at the problems of life: the deep belly laugh, hard won through facing adversity.

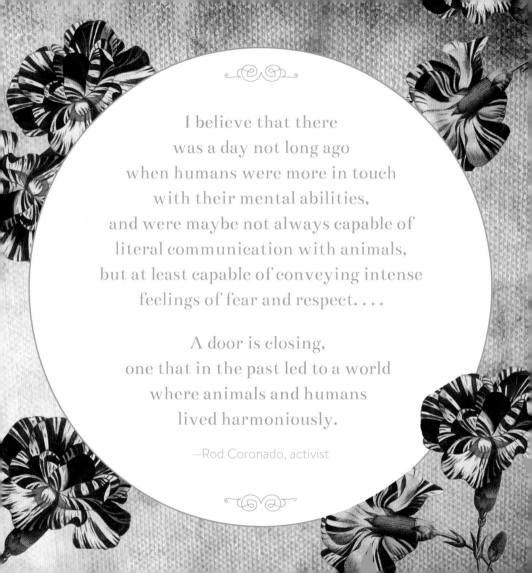

I believe that there
was a day not long ago
when humans were more in touch
with their mental abilities,
and were maybe not always capable of
literal communication with animals,
but at least capable of conveying intense
feelings of fear and respect. . . .

A door is closing,
one that in the past led to a world
where animals and humans
lived harmoniously.

—Rod Coronado, activist

This evening, think of all of the problems that you face now or have faced in the past: the relationship troubles, the financial messes, the family drama, the illnesses and deaths, the addictions and neuroses. Each one of these problems is a teacher in disguise, one of the grinding stones that wear down traces of egotism and narcissism. Mentally bow before each of these major life issues, and welcome each one as a teacher and friend. Resolve to learn the lesson behind each major problem, as this is the way to true freedom.

# Heart and Mind in Full Alignment

*Patriarchal masculinity teaches men that their sense of self and identity, their reason for being, resides in their capacity to dominate others. To change this males must critique and challenge male domination of the planet, of less powerful men, of women and children.*

*bell hooks, American author and feminist*

A spiritual practitioner can adopt materialism as a political strategy without adopting it as a metaphysical belief. Compassion demands that we accept that all people need food and housing, education and healthcare, and that the provision of such things is the minimum requirement for a just government. For reasons of conscience, we must object to any political or economic system that would place a premium on profit at the expense of the common people. Those who struggle for human dignity, for environmental quality, for the well-being of nonhuman animals, for an end to all forms of oppression, should be regarded as enlightened beings. To fail to engage in such a struggle is to exhibit laxity of mind and heart that is not conducive to liberation.

This evening, as you sit calmly in your meditation space, allow goodwill for all people to enter your heart. Cultivate a willingness to feel for the plight of others, to work to improve the lot of others, to change your habits of living to improve the world. Allow self-doubt and cynicism to fade away. Allow callous disregard to fade away. Feel your heart and mind, your compassion and intelligence, come into full alignment.

# Thoughts on
# the Inner Life

*Wherefore again and again does earth deserve / The name of mother given to her, for she / Herself alone created the human race / And at an appointed time herself produced / All animals that range in the mountains wide / And fowls of the air in all their varied forms.*

*Lucretius, Roman Epicurean poet*

Some version of the Golden Rule ("Do unto others as you would have them do unto you") exists in every religion of the world. And yet this principle seems to have had limited impact up to this point on world affairs. I believe the Golden Rule is the *beginning* of ethical reflection, the *gateway* to ethical reflection, and not the *sine qua non* of the ethical life. In order to make this rule worthwhile, we have to learn to inhabit difference, to see how the other person views things. We then have to care enough to risk changing our own beliefs, to cross over into a different point of view, perhaps permanently. We also have to turn the critical eye inward, to look at the failings of our own systems of belief, our own unconscious assumptions.

This evening, see in your mind's eye the type of inner life that you would like to have. Perhaps you can see yourself being more compassionate, more patient, or less irritable. Now ask yourself what it would take, what you would have to *change* about yourself, in order to make the desired state come more fully into reality. What beliefs, desires, thoughts, or opinions would you have to relinquish in order to make it to your goal? Mentally surrender whatever cherished mental habits you need to release.

# A Fast from the Mass Media

*I emphasize human ignorance which is, in my judgement,*
*the most certain faction in the school of the world.*

Michel de Montaigne, French philosopher and essayist

We construct our worlds on the basis of our previous experiences and the worldviews passed down to us by our parents and our society. Everything comes to consciousness prefiltered in this way: How then, can we experience anything anew? Just doing something different will not suffice, because of this prefiltering. To re-engage with the newness and freshness of the present, we have to somehow peel back the layers of ideology, of language, of tradition that prevent us from seeing. The inner silence, the deliberate refusal to label and categorize, represents at least the hope of fresh experience, the possibility of finding another way.

This evening, whether you sit in your own living room or on a ship in a distant port, set down the guardrails of your habitual vocabulary. Will your prefabricated explanations and descriptions to cease. Ask the language function to stop its games. Invite the ego to quiet itself. The jabber will continue, but try for a few minutes to find the loophole that allows you to dwell in the space before language.

# Reclaim Your Time

*Each of us seeks a treasure. It is elusive and difficult to achieve. It attracts us even when we aren't sure of its contents. The longing for it sustains us on rough and dangerous terrain. In the searching we already possess the sought-for.*

*Joan Puls, Franciscan nun and spiritual writer*

It has become fashionable these days to use the words "addictive" and "disruptive" as a compliment for a new technology or Internet startup. But let's think about what these words actually mean and decide whether we really think it is desirable to have people hooked on a technology or to disrupt an entire segment of the economy. If we turn people into zombies by getting them to play some electronic game, or if we kill a sector of the economy with a new app, is that really a good thing?

This evening, as you think about your own life, what has you *hooked*? What has you losing control of your own time, of your own psyche, of your own wallet? Can you dial back the hold that new technologies have on you? Imagine what you could do with an extra hour or two every day. Imagine what projects could be taken off the back burner and brought to completion.

# Bonds of Love

*By developing a vocabulary of feelings that allows us to
clearly and specifically name or identify our emotions, we can
connect more easily with one another. Allowing ourselves to be
vulnerable by expressing our feelings can help resolve conflicts.*

*Marshall B. Rosenberg,* Nonviolent Communication

The filaments of love, which seem so fragile and fleeting, actually hold reality together. Without love and attachment, there is no organizing or orienting perspective from which one could discern up from down, left from right, center from margin. Love and commitment, caring and community, make sense out of what would otherwise be chaos and dissolution. If we can piece together some sort of meaningful narrative, some perspective on life, we owe a debt of gratitude to those who cared for us, no matter how imperfectly.

This evening, as you breathe into the cave of the heart, feel that inner space expanding. Take the time to become aware of the outlines of your body. Become aware of the inner darkness over several minutes. Then see this inner space merging with the outer space, with the vast reaches of the stars. Feel a great sense of gratitude toward the mother who gave you birth, even if that relationship has been troubled. Receive care from the universe and vow to give care in return.

# Broken Yet Whole

*Ignorance conceals the pre-existent knowledge just as water plants cover over the surface of a pond. Clear away the plants and you have the water. You don't have to create it; it is already there.*

Sri Sai Baba of Shirdi, Hindu saint

At bottom, every person on earth wants to be loved and included, to be nurtured, to have the basic necessities of life. When people feel the need for love and caring violated, when they do not feel safe, when the necessities are unreachable, societies fracture into civil unrest. On a more interpersonal level, every broken personality trait stems from a misguided attempt to compensate for the absence of care in childhood. The first task of every society must be to care for the children. The second task must be to right the wrongs of the past.

This evening, as you gaze onto your own inner landscape, you may be quite aware of the broken places, of the fractured nature of your own mind and personality. As you watch your own inner turmoil, breathe deeply and relax. You do not need to improve yourself. You do not need to do more or be more than you are. Accept yourself and this moment as it is. Let go of the drive to achieve.

# Caring for the Next Generation

*Let Hari [the Lord] be the boat in which you cross over the sea of samsara [cyclic existence], patrolled by six deadly crocodiles—kama, krodha, lobha, mada, moha, and matsara: lust, anger, greed, conceit, delusion, and envy.*

Bhagavata Purana

The whole future of society depends on a child now playing with blocks. Society makes the child, and the child makes society. Children need us to *do* things for them, but they also just need us to be there for them. By caring for children, we build the future. Nothing could be more important than caring for children, and yet childcare is one of the most devalued activities in industrial societies. To make the world a more compassionate place, we must once again value the activity of caring for the next generation.

This evening, after sitting silently for ten to fifteen minutes, search your mind and heart for signs of a lack of generosity toward the young. Ask for an inspiration for one way in which you can perform an act of service that will make life better for future generations. When the insight comes, follow through on the inspiration: Do not be sparing of your time or money for this service. Pay no attention to the rewards and carry out your plans without delay.

# Spirit Guides

*There are painters who transform the sun to a yellow spot,*
*but there are others who with the help of their art and their*
*intelligence, transform a yellow spot into sun.*

Pablo Picasso, painter

Success should not be measured by the amount of time spent in corporate *bored* rooms or the make and model of one's automobile. Your soul does not give a damn whether you have the finest suit or watch. Your soul wants you to lie down in the grass and pick dandelions. It doesn't give a whit about the report you should be writing. No matter what your rational mind may say—*mind the 401(k), let's not get too excited here*—your heart will not settle for less than the fantastic, wonderful, adventurous life of your dreams.

The hard part is learning to separate the status symbols, what you are *supposed* to want, from the intuitive vision, what you *really* want. This is nigh unto impossible without mindfulness and meditation. It helps to have a spiritual guide, someone you can talk to, either in the flesh or in the astral realm. This evening, visualize the person you view as absolutely trustworthy: It could be Jesus, the Buddha, your guru, or your grandmother. After getting a bead on the appearance of that person and, more importantly, the feeling of that person's energy, go ahead and have a conversation. You will feel ridiculous, but do it anyway. Surprising clarity can be gained in this manner.

# The Original Wound

*Bear all you can, what you can, for power is bound to necessity.*

The Golden Verses of Pythagoras

Most of us make the same basic mistake, and maybe this is the problem with the psychotherapeutic worldview—that we try to fix, repair, mend, this original wound, supposedly originating from childhood. But what if there is no fix? What if there is no repair to be had because the brokenness is constitutive? If you think the point in life is to find some sort of cure, you will be sadly repeating the same cycle all over again. But if you can see that there is no cure, that the human condition (which is actually a subset of animal existence) is one that is perpetually bound to hardship, disappointment, and loss, then maybe you can find a small place of freedom.

This evening, take a look at your ego nature or personality. You need not destroy the ego nature in order to achieve liberation. You can be kind to yourself and even be self-confident; you only need to stop identifying with the ego or self. Observe it as though from the outside and do the ego no violence. Then you will be able to rise above it, to be free from its demands.

# Getting Through
# the Ups and Downs

*To stop your mind does not mean to stop the activities of mind.*
*It means your mind pervades your whole body.*

Shunryu Suzuki, Soto Zen priest

To experienced meditators, it can often feel like the practice has made no difference. But the practice of meditation is like the course correction when navigating by compass. Moving the direction of travel by one degree will lead to an entirely different destination over a long journey. When I think of my friends who meditate, I can readily see how the practice has made them more kind and compassionate. They may not be rich in worldly terms, but the lily doesn't need to be gilded.

Over the course of your practice, your enthusiasm will go through many ups and downs. Perhaps this evening you are feeling tired or bored. Do the practice anyway. Sit in silent listening for a few minutes at least. Watch your breath and watch the thoughts. Fill your heart and mind with love and caring; drive away the dark, aggressive thoughts. Return to the calm center of your being.

# Out of Control

*Taking a moment to look at the sky or taking a few seconds to abide
with the fluid energy of life, can give us a bigger perspective—that
the universe is vast, that we are a tiny dot in space, that, endless,
beginningless space is always available to us. Then we might
understand that our predicament is just a moment in time, and that
we have a choice to strengthen old habitual responses or to be free.*

*Pema Chödrön, American Buddhist author*

The ego nature makes a good servant but a poor master. The sense of self
provides comforting boundaries and allows for calculation of advantages and disadvantages. It allows for easy differentiation between self and other, which in turn atomizes the world into distinguishable objects. And yet, when the sense of separation from others gets too strong, it becomes easier to practice manipulation and act in uncaring ways. We have to learn to see the ego or personality as illusory and yet still recognize its proper place as an anchor to the world of objects and relationships.

This evening, as you have made it to the end of another day, take a few minutes to give thanks for the things that have gone well. Then ask for help for the situations that feel out of control. Take a few minutes to meditate on your chosen divinity or higher ideal. Close with meditation on peace.

# Father and Mother

*Nāda, is the Mantra name for the first going forth of Power which gathers itself together in massive strength (Ghanībhūta) as Bindu to create the universe, and which Bindu, as so creating, differentiates into a Trinity of Energies which are symbolized by A, U, M.*

Sir John Woodroffe (Arthur Avalon), Sanskritist

A look at history reveals two strands or themes: one the masculine, Father, thread, and the other the feminine, Mother, thread. The Father strand beats the drums of war and demands belief and achievement. The Mother strand, a lilting harmony or descant, asks for care and consideration, kindness and respect. These two strands exist in all people and have only tangentially to do with sex and gender, although men have historically been responsible for more atrocities in history. When the Father theme becomes too prevalent, war and strife, dogmatism and arrogance, result. The Mother thread has not often had the upper hand in historical memory, but it persists in the background, holding society together. The Father has bluster; the Mother has power.

Taking a look at your own life, has it been dominated by the Father or Mother pole? What could you do to bring balance to these forces? By entering deeply into meditation, you will be able to feel and hear these twin energies, perpetually spiraling around one another. If you listen deeply, you will be able to understand how they function in your life.

# The Library of Consciousness

*Live in your inner self alone / within your soul a world has grown, / the magic of veiled thoughts that might / be blinded by the outer light, / drowned in the noise of day, unheard ... / take in their song and speak no word.*

Fyodor Tyutchev, Russian poet

See how the frond of the fern unfurls, a branching fractal pathway in nature. Each being holds this seed-like store of secrets, ready to burst into fullness. This is no aberration but the usual way of things, this becoming, this flowering dehiscence. You, too, have your secrets and potentials, some of which will come into the light and make the world better. This, too, is your way: coming into fullness, becoming more participatory and open. You reach toward the sun, ever upward, ever more complete. This is becoming animal, becoming human, becoming divine.

This evening, your mind is an infinite storehouse, a magical library. Your mind is not *yours*, you see, but universal and open to all, coming from the All and returning to the All. Look deep within and see the treasures that await. See dark passageways and the crystal staircases. What treasures of the heart want and deserve to be birthed into the world? What will you take with you, and what will you leave behind? It is all a matter of choice.

Live in your inner self alone
within your soul a world has grown,
the magic of veiled thoughts that
might be blinded by the outer light,
drowned in the noise of day, unheard . . .
take in their song and speak no word.

—Fyodor Tyutchev, Russian poet

# Mantra and Pranayama

*The mind of God . . . is cosmic music, the music of strings*
*resonating through 11 dimensional hyperspace.*

*Michio Kaku, theoretical physicist*

After performing *puja* (ritual worship) or chanting is a good time to do mindfulness meditation. Mantras take away the bad thoughts and replace them with good thoughts, so that the atmosphere becomes conducive to contemplation. The vibratory nature of the mantras cleanses and opens the chakras so that higher states of consciousness can be reached more easily. Chanting and mindfulness naturally complement one another: We chant mindfully just as we can eat mindfully or walk mindfully. In this way, every aspect of life becomes an offering to the divine or a participation in the Buddha nature.

This evening, begin your practice with a recitation of your favorite scripture or saying a mala of your favorite mantra. Then begin your silent meditation with four rounds of breath work. If you are not trained in pranayama, try the practice recommended in the *Kashyāpa Sutras*. Breathe in for four counts, hold for sixteen counts, and breathe out for eight counts. Hold for two counts on the exhalation, then repeat. This same routine can be done using alternate nostril breathing, holding the closed nostril with the Vishnu mudra. You can then return to a deeper version of your normal breathing for the remainder of your mindfulness practice.

# Meditation on Imagery

*Clear and sweet is my soul, and clear and sweet is all that is not my soul.*
*Lack one lacks both, and the unseen is proved by the seen.*

*Walt Whitman, American poet*

Perhaps you are drawn to Eastern philosophy but consider yourself an atheist. This need not be an obstacle to practice. Certain strands of Hinduism and Buddhism are more atheistic in nature, and the theistic strands may be taken as metaphorical in nature. As you learn more about the iconography of the deities, you will see that each and every weapon and ornament of the gods has a symbolic meaning. The battle axe stands for good actions, the spear stands for the prick of conscience, the bowl of sweets stands for the good things in life, and so forth. The images of the Buddhas and bodhisattvas similarly have deep symbolism.

This evening, choose a picture of a deity, saint, or other revered figure to focus your meditation. Concentrate upon the image with your eyes open until it becomes etched in your consciousness, so that you can see each detail with your eyes closed. Then sit in silent adoration for as much time as you have available. If you wish, you may then enter into a conversation with the spiritual guide. Just try to do more listening than speaking, and always err on the side of silence.

# Heartbreaking Love

*Unbreakable, O Lord, / Is the love that binds me to You: /*
*Like a diamond, / It breaks the hammer that strikes it.*

*Mirabai, Hindu saint*

When we experience some heartbreak in life, which will certainly occur to everyone at some point, we have two choices. We can withdraw from life and anesthetize the pain, or we can go out there again and meet life with boldness. Either way leads to more pain. But the pain that has been freely chosen has less sting and has the benefit of shared suffering, being in community with others who share a similar fate. By withdrawing from the world and seeking to dull the pain, we then have to experience it alone, which is much more difficult.

This evening, as you breathe deeply, watch the play of thoughts as they flit through your mind. You may be mentally replaying the events of the day or wondering about what might happen tomorrow. Allow your consciousness to move down the axis of the body into the darkness of the chest cavity. Become aware of this space and allow it to expand. Allow the boundaries of your body to become permeable to your surroundings. Then allow your awareness to expand in all directions, so that it includes the outdoors and the vastness of space. When you are ready, come back down into your body and return to watching the breath.

# Toward a New Consciousness

*Earth cannot be changed for the better unless the consciousness of individuals is changed first. We pledge to increase our awareness by disciplining our minds, by meditation, by prayer, or by positive thinking. Without risk and a readiness to sacrifice there can be no fundamental change in our situation. Therefore we commit ourselves to this global ethic, to understanding one another, and to socially beneficial, peace-fostering, and nature-friendly ways of life.*

*Parliament of the World's Religions, "Declaration Toward a Global Ethic"*

Stop thinking so much about what other people have done to you, how they have hindered you and failed to support you. Stop thinking so much about how things have been unfair, how you haven't gotten the credit that you deserve. The real questions are: When will you stop torturing yourself? When will you be more kind to yourself? When will you *let things be*? When will you "let sleeping dogs lie," as they say in my native South? When will you allow yourself to be what you want to be, what you *are*?

This evening, as you breathe deeply into the cave of the heart, allow yourself to be as you are. Everything, at this moment, is exactly as it should be. You do not need to correct any thought that may arise. You have nothing deficient or sinful within yourself. Everything coming into being at this moment is exactly and completely perfect and could not have been otherwise. Rest here in this perfection, in this completeness, in this exhalation and inhalation of the divine breath.

# Loving and Caring

*Love is more than a feeling. It is active and transitive. . . .*
*Love is what I do to create this sense of feeling cared for.*
*It is independent of my personal feelings.*

*Morton T. Kelsey, Episcopal priest*

As you look out at the universe, you will see nothing but prior conditions giving rise to later conditions, so that the present is fully determined by what went before. And yet, somehow, mysteriously, we can still choose. The space of freedom is not as large as some might think—definitely not absolute, but it is still there, this small pocket of flux and possibility arising only in this moment. We have to learn how to work with this tiny opening of possibility, to make something beautiful of our lives, not only for ourselves, but for all beings.

This evening, ask yourself if your approach to life is really serving yourself and others. As you breathe deeply and become more present to this moment, build an intense feeling of care and concern for yourself, for your family and relations, and for all creatures. Allow this feeling of care and concern to arise to a crescendo, to the point where it hurts, to the point where it feels your heart might break for love. Hold this feeling for as long as you can, and when you come back to ordinary awareness, see if your mental and emotional space does not feel expanded.

# The Power of Attention

*Those skilled in war subdue the enemy's army without battle.*

Sun Tzu, Chinese military strategist

You may be feeling sad and disappointed now, as though you had lived for nothing. Maybe you did something you regret or feel that you have not done enough in life. Maybe you have let others down or let yourself down. Maybe you are comparing yourself to others and feel like you do not measure up. Just remember that change characterizes everything under the sun, which means that whatever is bothering you will pass. Remember also that this moment is absolutely new and unique in the history of the universe, and that you can decisively break with the past. If you are patient, everything can change for you, as the old patterns are overwritten with new ones.

There is no point in pretending that you have no negative feelings or dark thoughts, but you need not indulge them or go along with them. Simply sit this evening and watch the thoughts and feelings, whatever they may be. Attend to them, pay attention to them. You don't have to give them what they want: just observe. The more your attention skills improve, the weaker these negative thoughts will be. This evening, endeavor to outlast the negative thoughts.

# Strength of the Heart

*The divine names are the same / as that which they name / They are nothing but he / But they demand the realities / which they express / And the realities that they demand / are nothing other than the world.*

*Ibn Arabi, Sufi mystic*

When you live according to your personal integrity, when you value the practices that give meaning to your own life and the lives of others, you make it easier for others to do the same. When other people see you living with compassion toward other people and nonhuman animals, when they see you meditating and taking care of yourself, when they see you wisely managing time and resources, they cannot help but be inspired. Let us be those who step off the treadmill of meaningless activity, who demand a sane and peaceful way of life, who redirect resources toward the young and the marginalized. Mindfulness can be a personal practice, but it can also be a force for social transformation.

This evening, as you breathe into your heart center, feel your intuitive awareness growing stronger. You will not need an a, b, or c plan of action. As you listen more deeply to your own heart, your conscience will grow stronger. You will no longer be able to willingly hurt living things. You will no longer accept petty justifications for cruelty directed against any living being. As peace fills your own heart this evening, it radiates out into the world, to every life that touches your own.

# Taking Shelter in Karma

*No effort ever goes to waste in selfless service, and there is no*
*adverse effect. Even a little practice of this discipline protects*
*one from the cycle of repeated birth and death.*

*Bhagavad Gita 2.40*

Our cynical world dismisses any idea as "utopian" that would give people a living wage, that would make for a cleaner environment, that would prevent exploitation of workers or the earth. In short, any idea that might jeopardize the underlying motive of greed is dismissed as impractical, while anything that makes money is regarded as right and good. Such an inversion of truth cannot last long and will not be the basis for a sustainable society or a viable world order. As you begin to practice meditation more regularly, you will become more attuned to this strange inversion of moral values and become more comfortable with speaking against it.

This evening, take comfort in the idea that the law of karma is alive and working. Take shelter in this law, and reorder your mind and heart according to its dictates. Those who live according to this law will be protected by it, while those who go against it will suffer. As you will for the good of all beings, you promote your own good as well. Dwell here in this space of universal goodwill; allow it to transform your thoughts and affections.

# The Keys of Time

*There's nothing worse for a forest than to have all the trees be the same.*

*Ken Kesey, American writer*

Every moment holds a new potential for spiritual awakening. We carry with us this terrible weight of the history of the world, of our own personal histories, but the past does not have the final say. Right now you can snap out of the gray tunnel of the past and see this moment in all of its vividness and uniqueness. Right now you can break free from the haze and grime of habitual thought and move into the clear light of present awareness. Give yourself this chance for freedom, to set down the burden of *how things have always been* and open yourself to *what may be.*

As you breathe into this present, feel your consciousness of time expanding. Feel the duration and thickness of this second, this minute. As you set aside all other thoughts, concentrate on this time as it expands before your mind's eye. See that you hold the keys of time: You can make this moment last or you can throw it away. Stay with the expansion of this moment—live into this present with everything that you have. Know that you always have the ability to step into the lived duration of the present.

# Have No Enemies

*Fearing God means primarily fearing for the other.*

Emmanuel Levinas, French philosopher

If over 7 billion people are to live together on the same planet peacefully, certain ideas will just have to die or be drastically downgraded. We must put other people above pride of nation and creed. We must put planet ahead of profit. We must prioritize concord over combat. All of these would be vast departures from the modern era, and they require huge changes in society (particularly in the wealthy, industrialized nations of the West). But change must begin somewhere, and it begins with the right thinking, feeling, and acting of people of conscience.

This evening, as you bring a close to your day, open your heart and mind to other people, who may live halfway around the world, who may practice a different religion and speak another language. Resolve to have no enemies, not even those whom your government or party tell you that you should fear. See no group of people as an inherent threat to you or your way of life. Feel in your heart a growing resolve to believe in peace and work for peace.

# Bodily Awareness

*Most men, it appears to me, do not care for Nature, and would*
*sell their share in all her beauty, for as long as they may live,*
*for a stated and not very large sum. Thank God they cannot*
*yet fly and lay waste the sky as well as the earth! We are safe*
*on that side for the present. It is for the very reason that*
*some do not care for these things that we need to combine to*
*protect all from the vandalism of a few.*

*Henry David Thoreau, American transcendentalist author*

We live much of our lives disconnected from bodily awareness, more concerned with screen time than the dream time. We cannot bypass bodily consciousness on the way to "higher" states, since the body is the vehicle through which we approach the divine. When we close our eyes to meditate, when we breathe deeply, we become aware of the body. The hairs on the skin stand erect, the spine lengthens. We become aware of the rushing of blood. If we can get still enough, we become aware of the heartbeat. We see the dance of lights behind the eyes.

This evening, as you close your eyes in meditation, let the interior dialogue melt into close observation of the body and its states. Move your awareness down the spinal axis, from the crown of the head to the sacrum, very slowly and deliberately, surveying each sensation along the way. Then move back up the spinal axis again, allowing your awareness to rest at the heart center or between the eyes. As you breathe in, picture the breath entering the bottom of the spine. As you breathe out, picture the breath flowing out of the crown of your head. This will provide a point of entry into awareness of the kundalini energy.

# Divine Madness

*Blank walls make blank people.*

*Anonymous graffiti, Athens, Greece*

Your teachers and guides haven't told you everything and can't tell you everything, but they have given you enough and more than enough to get started. You already know the way to the place where you are going. The maps are written on the bark of trees. The signposts can be seen in the wanderings of ants, in the phosphorescent glow of foliage at dusk. I could speak gibberish to you, and you would still grasp the meaning. The heart knows its homecoming, and the lover knows the beloved. "*Hum!*," the goddess says, and she reduces the demons to dust.

This evening, notice in your mind that little voice that holds you back just when you start getting somewhere in your practice. Just when the silence becomes uncomfortable, just beyond the boundaries of normal consciousness, the overcautious voice pulls back. What is your overcautious voice saying this evening? Maybe it tells you to get a sandwich, turn on the television, or read a book. Try to resist this voice of distraction just a little longer, and a little longer.

# Unaltered State

*Where seekest thou? That freedom, friend, this world / Nor that can give. In books and temples, vain / Thy search. Thine only is the hand that holds / The rope that drags thee on.*

Swami Vivekananda, founder, Ramakrishna Math and Ramakrishna Mission

We think of mindfulness and meditation as inducing altered states of consciousness, but these states are only altered from the reference point of typical consciousness, which is actually quite altered in itself. Mindfulness is a return to baseline clarity and calm. It is a process of peeling back the layers of conceptual thought and the associated emotions to deep attention and observation. Mindfulness continuously and actively sets aside preconceived notions about life and reality in the effort to approach the present directly and unencumbered. Achieving this goal, even for a second or two, brings great peace.

*Yoga* comes from the same root as *yoke*. This evening, bind together, yoke together, your mind, your body, and your breath. Have nothing else to do but sit calmly in this moment. As the mind wanders, gently bring it back to center. No matter how attractive the thoughts might be, avoid inquiring into them in the sense of being drawn into a monologue. Notice the thoughts, but do not prolong them. Try to pay attention to the spaces between the thoughts, to the space between breaths. Lengthen and slow the process of breathing and thinking, always alert and attentive.

# Cooperation and Evolution

*Cooperation is part of nature, down to the cellular level. The reason why is simple, according to evolutionary biologists: Cooperation is one of the most important and beneficial behaviors on Earth. We literally would not be here without it.*

Jeremy Adam Smith and Alex Dixon, science writers

I once knew a farmer who had a good-sized herd of cows on his property in rural Georgia. He kept goldfish in the watering trough for his cows. The goldfish kept the algae in the trough from getting out of control, which kept the cows supplied with clean drinking water. It saved my farmer friend a lot of labor as well, because he didn't have to continually clean the water tanks. Mutually beneficial relationships like this persist everywhere in nature and in human society alike, only we have been conditioned not to see them because we are so indoctrinated into the gospel of greed and competition.

As you settle into your evening meditation space and do your breathing exercises, let go of the need to protect "me and mine." Allow yourself to transgress the prevailing idea that we live in a "dog eat dog" world. Meditate for a few minutes on the ideas of trust and mutuality. Take note of any resistance that you have to this way of being. You need not pressure yourself or judge yourself for any thoughts that arise in response.

## Cooperation

is part of nature,
down to the cellular level.
The reason why is simple,
according to evolutionary biologists:

COOPERATION IS ONE OF THE MOST IMPORTANT
AND BENEFICIAL BEHAVIORS ON EARTH.

We literally would not
be here without it.

—Jeremy Adam Smith and
Alex Dixon, science writers

# Logging Off

*Existence in late capitalism is a permanent rite of initiation. Everyone must show that they identify wholeheartedly with the power which beats them.*

Max Horkheimer and Theodor W. Adorno, critical theorists

We are the most measured, tagged, and observed people in the course of human history. Our every movement is tracked wirelessly. We voluntarily keep track of money spent, calories consumed, steps taken. We have photos and video of nearly every day of our lives. It is only natural to feel a sense of alarm and anxiety at these rapid developments, and yet we are made to feel as though this were all quite normal and even fun. The unacknowledged pressure to conform to this information regime is ever present and far from benign. The challenge that this regime presents to would-be meditators is to find a space of solitude and quiet in a world of noise, to find surrender and acceptance in a world driven mad with measurement.

This evening, refrain from the usual status updates. Log off the Internet and put down your electronic devices. Sit and do nothing at all, or read a book if you must. Avoid entertainment. Resist the urge to read the news. If you must eat something, make it simple. Do everything slowly and easily. Sit outside awhile. Then sit inside. Pay attention to your world. Laugh. See how long you can keep up this purposeful indolence.

# Slow Media

*The sage acts but does not possess, completes his work but does not dwell on it. In this fashion, he has no desire to display his worth.*

Tao Te Ching

What strikes me lately about the Internet is just how predictable it all can be, in spite of all the talk of innovation and disruption. I know what the headlines will be at my favorite news and commentary sites before I even visit them. The Facebook posts vary, but they also have a certain standardized format: the vacation pic, the food pic, the humble brag, the various complaints, the political digs (mostly preaching to the choir). I actually love all of my Facebook friends, but the medium gets in the way. Social media becomes a substitute for actual conversation, for the face-to-face encounter. So what makes it all so addictive? I'm not sure really, but there I go: click, scroll down, click, click.

The slow-food movement gets us all thinking about our eating habits, but what about slow media? This evening, spend some time writing in your journal. Make a collage or a zine. Write a poem. Plunk on your guitar or piano. Rant and rave, but do it in real time. Do it, just this once, if only as a reminder of how much things have changed.

# Breaking Through Stereotypes

*Our sense of reality here is an entire delusion; we know nothing of things, of people, as they are; all that we know of them are the impressions they make on our senses, and the conclusions, often erroneous, which our reason deduces from the aggregate of these impressions.*

*Annie Besant, British theosophist*

There will always be politicians and religious leaders who seek to score cheap points by denigrating an "outside" group. Such tactics appeal to our base instincts and tribal urges. They get us to ignore the real causes of any problems in society and get us to scapegoat the defenseless other. This tactic should be familiar by now, but somehow it keeps working. The mindfulness-based practitioner commits to avoiding rhetorical violence that would pit one group in society against another. Mindfulness requires vigilance of mind and heart and will not accept emotion without intelligence or vice versa.

Cultural stereotypes are inimical to mindfulness, as they prevent us from attending to the person as an individual. This evening, see if you can meditate with eyes open in a public place. Watch people as they play, as they come home from work, as they shop and dine. If any stereotypes arise in your mind, let them go. Attend to each person as an individual at a particular place and time. Observe without commenting.

# Avoiding Harshness in Speech

*The ranges and limits [of the individual consciousness] can be so widened as to be coextensive with the whole universe—can even be entirely transcended by following a path of living, behavior, and action that is in harmony with the All, with the universal movement, with the Self and Spirit of the All.*

J.C. Chatterji, *Vedic scholar*

Each person, as a multifaceted being, has many possible truths, many possible descriptions that could be called accurate. We can speak harsh truths about each other and about ourselves, but these harsh truths act as irritants, as weapons, that lead to further wounding and alienation. Harsh truths ultimately lead to increased defense mechanisms and neurotic behavior. We should avoid these harsh truths and try to speak the good words that heal and mend, not to sugarcoat reality but out of a sense of solidarity and fellowship. We should speak kindly to each other, not in a condescending way but just to be good and decent.

This evening, you may find yourself speaking harsh words about yourself. Observe that inner dialogue, which may be more raw than anything you would say aloud: "I am such a loser. Why can't I get my act together?" Such overstatements may be accompanied by mental "evidence" that purports to support the negative talk, but this, too, is largely overblown or fabricated. Notice the ways in which you act as a prosecuting attorney against yourself. Stepping outside of this habit is difficult, but just noticing it is the first step.

# Surrender to Reality

*In meditative prayer, one thinks and speaks not only*
*with his mind and lips, but in a certain sense with*
*his whole being. Prayer is then not just a formula of*
*words, or a series of desires springing up in the heart—*
*it is the orientation of our whole body, mind and spirit*
*to God in silence, attention, and adoration.*

Thomas Merton, *Trappist monk*

The Appalachian Mountains of my childhood look like smooth, green and blue waves, but they can be deceptively tough for hikers and backpackers. The single track of the Appalachian Trail is only a foot wide, but it contains many switchbacks and false summits as it winds its way from Georgia to Maine. Many hikers have also been unprepared for the unexpected cold and snows along the route or have been forced to turn back because of a busted knee or turned ankle. Nature teaches us with its opposites: its highs and lows, its unexpected turns, its unpredictable moods.

This evening, perhaps you have encountered some situation in life that will not bend to your plans. Perhaps you have doggedly pursued a course of action that won't seem to work. Perhaps it has taken a toll on your physical and mental health. This evening, as you breathe deeply into your heart center, offer the situation up to your idea of a higher power. Let go of your plans, let go of all frustration. Surrender to reality, to things as they are, and open yourself to a softer way, a more adaptive way, a different way. Be open to new insights and a new course of action.

# The Silent Witness

*He who knows God as the Life of life, the Eye of the
eye, the Ear of the ear, the Mind of the mind, he indeed
comprehends fully the Cause of all causes.*

Brihadaranyaka Upanishad

We are taught from a young age to not be lazy, to go to school and work hard, to achieve and believe, and all sorts of other nuggets of wisdom from Successories posters. None of this advice is especially wrong, but maybe the dosage is too high or we are conditioned to expect unrealistic results. Life just sucks sometimes. It is hard—*really hard*—to just keep your head above water. Then to add on top of that the continuous need for self-improvement, and it's just too much to expect. Sometimes the best thing that you can do is to say *no* to the next big gimmick to change your life.

This evening, let go of the need to make your life better, bigger, faster, and more. Accept your financial difficulties, your troubled emotions, your fraught relationships—all of it. Be the silent witness to the drama unfolding around you. Inhale deep calm and tranquility. Do not rise to the bait of thinking that you have to be someone other than who you are at this place and time. Do not punish yourself for having a past, for making mistakes, for, well, living. Just let events unfold naturally, one thing at a time.

# Pain and Discomfort
# As Friends

*In cultures where asceticism developed and was practiced, people knew that one can suffocate when every option is a readily available one. Without self-limitation, without fixed boundaries—like those given in creation between day and night, summer and winter, being young and growing old—life loses its humanness. Asceticism means to renounce at least for periods of time the options that present themselves.*

Dorothee Soelle, theologian and activist

Beware of anyone who tells you that a problem, whether personal, national, or geopolitical, can be solved easily and painlessly. Everything good in the social world has been achieved through hard struggle, usually through generations, on the part of many committed individuals. The prosperity and well-being you have experienced personally has also come at the cost of great sacrifice on the part of previous generations and those now living. Beware the con artists who offer easy fixes and quick remedies. They are legion, and they are looking to line their own pockets and achieve power for themselves.

This evening, as you settle your mind and heart, probe your willingness to endure discomfort. Perhaps you find it difficult to set everything else aside to have a few minutes of peace. Perhaps you are having physical pain of some sort as you endeavor to sit with upright posture and breathe deeply. Be mindful of pain and discomfort; label them as friends and not enemies. Sit with them quietly and notice them. Without these friends, nothing good can come to you.

# Happiness and Desire

*A sampling of Forbes magazine's "richest Americans" has happiness scores identical with those of the Pennsylvania Amish and only a whisker above those of Swedes, not to mention Masai tribesmen. The "life satisfaction" of pavement dwellers—that is, homeless people—in Calcutta was among the lowest recorded, but it almost doubled when they moved into a slum, at which point they were basically as satisfied with their lives as a sample of college students drawn from forty-seven nations.*

Bill McKibben, environmental activist

Suppose I secure wealth and fame, but I do nothing to lift my fellow human beings out of poverty and ignorance. I will have failed to live a just life. Suppose I live in a huge mansion on a private island, but I lose the ability to exercise my conscience. I will have gained nothing. Suppose everyone thinks of me as a fabulous and entertaining person, but I have not spoken on behalf of the earth and the nonhuman creatures. My life would be a fraud. History is one long series of atrocities against indigenous peoples, against racial, religious, and political minorities. It is a history of exploitation of the earth and living things. But the future need not be the same as the past: It is, after all, the future.

Perhaps you nurture in your heart a desire for wealth and fame, property and privilege. It's okay, we all do from time to time. See this grasping nature as it arises in your mind and heart. Investigate it without being held by it. See if you can loosen the desire this evening, if only a little bit. See if you can trust, if only for a few minutes, that your needs will be satisfied. See that tiny glimmer of trust in the benevolence of the universe: Hold on to that little place of trust and watch it expand.

# The Paradox of
# Inside and Outside

*I, the reduced "human Ego" ("psychophysical" Ego), am constituted, accordingly, as a member of the "world" with a multiplicity of "objects outside me." But I myself constitute all this in my "psyche" and and bear it intentionally within me.*

Edmund Husserl, founder of phenomenological philosophy

The challenge for extroverted people is to learn to sit quietly and listen. The challenge for introverted people is to share feelings and intentions with others. Both tasks require courage and discernment. Both require stepping outside of our comfort zones. To live together on an interpersonal level requires noticing our boundaries and working to open a space of hospitality on that boundary. Living together also requires a critical examination of the signals that we send to others, to make sure that we are communicating in a way that honors our best intentions.

As you sit and breathe deeply, notice the boundaries between your body and the "outside." Now notice your internal perception of space. Form a picture of the room in which you are seated without opening your eyes. Notice a certain ambivalence here: What does it mean for the "outside" to be on the "inside"? See how these distinctions blur in the action of the mind.

# The Inner Wellspring

*The essence of meditation is stillness in the midst of activity. . . . In meditation, we discover very quickly just how busy our minds usually are. But, also in meditation, we have the opportunity to taste the stillness that is always here in the midst of unending movement and change.*

Steve Hagen, Zen priest

As I respect your boundaries, I come home to myself. As I let go of my grasping nature as it pertains to you, I find in myself untapped potential. As long as I need you, I cannot love you in a mature way. It is only as I become my full self that I can let you be yours. Of course, the self is a construction, but it must become more broad and expansive as we grow into selflessness. At that point, there is no longer a binary between self and other: just this one limitless expanse of which we all partake.

This evening, as you enter into this safe space and time of contemplation, do your usual preliminary activities of deep breathing and mantra practice. Then think about what you need from others, what you try to get from them. Can you let go of those needs and demands? Can you look within to find your sufficiency? See that deep wellspring of strength and vitality arising in your heart. See it as totally reliable and endless, a constant source of strength and well-being.

# Giving Thanks for Predecessors

*Friendship . . . is more necessary in bad fortune, . . .*
*but it is more noble in good fortune.*

Aristotle, Greek philosopher

The world does not change on its own, but by the actions of men and women of conscience down through the ages who have made society more just and inclusive. Those living today can choose to expand their legacy and so increase the principle on which the interest is due, or they can squander the inheritance and lead society down the path to ruin. Those of us who have been given the privilege of life and freedom can choose to be small people, obsessed with only self-preservation, or we can be giants, living as much as possible into our ideals of virtue and justice. We can live according to the better angels of our nature or according to the most vicious tendencies.

This evening, as you settle into your seat of meditation, touch the earth in front of you and say a prayer for stability and good foundation. Give thanks to those who came before you, who made your life possible. Ask for their blessing to become a voice for goodness and justice in the world. Pray for the strength to hold to the truth, to elevate humankind, and protect the earth. Feel this communion of people down through the ages who long for a better life for future generations.

# Animal Body, Animal Mind

*To err is human, to forgive canine.*

*Anonymous*

Some of my favorite videos on YouTube are of people who make prostheses for disabled animals. When I see someone making a wheelchair for a paraplegic dog out of tinker toys and LEGO bricks, it somehow gives me hope for humanity. Of course, I know that millions of dogs and cats are still euthanized each year, but someone cared enough about that one animal to give it back its mobility. Someone cared for an animal that would have been drowned or shot a couple of decades ago. If the humane sentiment spreads far enough and wide enough, maybe there is hope that we can live on planet earth in a more sane and holistic way.

We are all, in one way or another, injured animals, whether those wounds are physical or mental. This evening, as you settle into your space of meditation, live into your own animal body, your own animal mind. Feel the respiring lungs congressing with the atmosphere, the hairs of your arms standing on end. Feel the creaturely nature of your limbs and viscera. Notice the craving for food, for comfort, for sex. Become animal, not so that you can transcend the animal, but so that you know yourself more fully. Do not seek to distance yourself from nature but to become part of it, to merge with it.

# Perfection in This Moment

*The goal to be reached is the mind's insight into what knowing is. Impatience asks for the impossible, wants to reach the goal without the means of getting there. The length of the journey has to be borne with, for every moment is necessary.*

G.W.F. Hegel, German idealist philosopher

Motivational literature usually recommends fantasizing some version of an Ideal Future Self, followed by goal-setting exercises, complete with due dates and checklists. In some cases and for some people, this approach may work. Let's say you get the dream job or the six- or seven-figure income or the beachfront property or the hundred-pound weight loss. Problem solved, right? Well, no, because you have never accepted yourself as is, have never lived in proximity, in familiarity with your normal waking consciousness and your everyday life. So your headspace is always in the imaginary future or in the idealized image, never right here.

Perhaps you have some scenario of an Ideal Future Self, one that you have strived to reach for years. Perhaps you have invested considerable amounts of time and money into realizing that fantasy. Most likely, at least some aspects of your vision have come true. See if you can try, just

The goal to be reached
is the mind's insight into
what KNOWING is.

*Impatience asks for the impossible,*
*wants to reach the goal without*
*the means of getting there.*

The length of the journey
has to be borne with, for
EVERY MOMENT IS NECESSARY.

—G.W.F. Hegel, German
idealist philosopher

for the space of your meditation this evening, to surrender that image of an Ideal Future Self. Embrace, if only for a few minutes, your life exactly as it is at this moment. You can always go back to striving later, but, just for these few minutes, give yourself a break. You are so good and so beautiful and perfect exactly the way you are.

# The Home and the Heart's Desire

*The house shelters daydreaming, the house protects the dreamer, the house allows one to dream in peace. . . . The values that belong to daydreaming mark humanity in its depths.*

Gaston Bachelard, French philosopher

Traveling, whether across town or to another continent, allows one to experience home more fully, not only the comforts of home but also the otherness of home, the deliberate choices that one has made in order to craft this particular nest. When we return home, it is as though the décor belonged to someone else who is seen for the first time. Our homes project our plans and programs, our desires and longings, the ways that we see ourselves and the ways that we want to be seen. By knowing the home, we know what is on our own minds.

As you walk through your home this evening, look for the little clues all around you about your heart's desire. You may see evidence of places you want to visit, subjects you would like to study, old friends whom you miss, and the like. Hold these sacred yearnings in your mind and heart as you do your evening meditation. Then take a few small action steps that will bring your vision into reality.

# Holding Future Generations in the Heart

*Only little men fear little writings.*

Pierre Beaumarchais, French dramatist

It can be easy to feel small and insignificant in the face of all of the great problems facing humanity, which can cause paralysis of the will. But every great movement in history, whether political, religious, or cultural, made waves not because of the efforts of lone heroic individuals but because of the small efforts of many individuals. The transition to a dharmic society, a just society, a mindful society, will also occur because of the dispersed efforts of millions. As we multiply our efforts, we join our individual wills to the mind of Nature, which cares for the well-being of all.

This evening, as you breathe deeply into the heart center, see there in the heart the future generations, the untold billions who will come after you. See the people, but also see the forests and animals, the fish and the seas, the tiny microbes and the tallest mountains. Allow your concern for them to change your mind, to change your affections, to govern your life. Know that even beneath the level of your conscious mind, in ways that you cannot now understand, your life and priorities are being reordered. Because of these minutes of contemplation today, your life will not be the same.

# Make Time for Spiritual Reflection

*When will I be mad with love, when will I drown in the ocean of*
*happiness? And become mad myself, and make everyone mad?*
*And take shelter in the lotus feet of Krishna?*

*Devotional song from Vrindavan, India*

We tend to give only our spare minutes to meditation and spirituality. Think about the message that this sends: that we don't really care about the cultivation of the mind, that we prefer to let things be haphazard, that we prefer to be governed by the emotions and senses. Even late in the day, we can still be stingy with our time and resources, preferring mindless entertainment to the needs of the spirit. And then we wonder why we find life to be so tedious and unsatisfying.

This evening, take for yourself some time apart from housework and chores, from news and entertainment. Go off by yourself for your meditation if you can. If not, just maintain internal quiet as much as possible. Allow calm and quiet to be your companion. Again, if you cannot control your external environment, cultivate quiet within.

# Strengthening the Attentive Mind

*A deeply receptive mode is passive. There is a relaxation or giving up of subjectness. But this passivity, the giving way to the other as subject, is willed or acceded to by the receptive agent. The mind remains, or may remain, remarkably active, but instrumental striving is suspended.*

Nel Noddings and Paul Shore, educational theorists

Speaking in a rough, schematic sense, we have an active, acquisitive, propositional movement of consciousness, the part of our minds that carries out plans and looks for solutions. Then we also have a sensitive, responsive, attentive mode of consciousness that primarily absorbs its surroundings, noticing things in all of their particularity and texture. Our society has overdeveloped and overrewarded the first kind of consciousness while allowing the second kind of consciousness to atrophy. As a result, we can no longer adequately pay attention to the world around us, which comes to seem bland and colorless.

To strengthen the attentive mind, you must learn to get comfortable with silence, with what might at first be perceived as an absence of stimulation. This evening, sit in silence for a predetermined period of time, something that seems difficult to you and yet not impossible. Try twenty, forty, or sixty minutes of silent listening.

# Stamina for the Long Journey

*The true frontier for humanity is life on Earth—its exploration and the transport of knowledge about it into science, art, and practical affairs. . . . 90 percent or more of the species of plants, animals, and microorganisms lack even so much as a scientific name; each of the species is immensely old by human standards; . . . life around us exceeds in complexity and beauty anything else humanity is ever likely to encounter.*

E.O. Wilson, entomologist, conservationist, and author

Humanity has only a few short decades to successfully navigate a perilous path strewn with traps that could lead to annihilation. We still have enough nuclear weapons on the earth to destroy the earth thousands of times over. Climate change threatens catastrophic storms, destruction of food crops, and reduction in water supply that could affect billions. Wealth and power are concentrated into the hands of the few, a global elite who seem to care nothing about people or planet. And yet there is still hope: While we still have breath, we can fight for a better tomorrow.

Meditation and mindfulness supply the stamina, the wherewithal to keep going even in the face of depressing trends. This evening, allow your breath to fill you with renewed purpose and strength. Patiently wait before the cosmos, ready to receive new insight. Sit attentively, knowing that you do so not just for yourself but for all those who share the earth with you. Renounce all selfish motives and open your heart to the divine mystery.

# Letting Go of Control

*Acceptance allows us to use our pain as a means of growth.*

Donna Miesbach, meditation and yoga instructor

We like to believe that we are in control of our own lives, but the idea of a locus of control, residing in the mind or in the personality, is an illusion. We can no more control our own lives than we can control a hurricane. To be sure, there are more placid periods, just as there is an eye in a storm. The fact is that everything can spiral out of control at any time, even when we have the best organizational schemes, the best preparation. The trick is to find calm despite this basic unpredictability.

This evening, as you settle into your meditation space, surrender the idea that you can plan for all contingencies. Let go of the idea that you are the master of your own destiny. Let go of the ego tendency that tells you that you control events. Surrender to the chaotic nature of the universe, and give yourself to its radical flux. See yourself as an extension of nature, and release your personal will.

# In the Dry Places

*Even as wax is melted before the face of the fire, so is the soul enfeebled by praise, and loses the toughness of its virtues.*

*Syncletica, Christian Desert Mother*

Once one of the *sadhakas* (aspirants) had taken a *sankalpa* (vow) to say a particular set of divine names over a period of several months. He got about two thirds of the way through the *sankalpa*, and the divine names (in this case, the Lalita Trishati, some names for the Goddess) became very dry to this seeker, where they had been sweet and nourishing at the beginning. Our guru, Swamiji, said to the *sadhaka*, "It is when the mantras are dull and dry that they are the most important: It is then that they are doing the most good." It occurred to me that only the dry period can scrub away our tendencies to crave exciting experiences.

Perhaps this evening you feel no desire to say mantras, to read scripture, to pray or meditate. Perhaps you just want to flop on the couch and do nothing. That is fine, all well and good, but try to muster the strength to do a few minutes of meditation first. As you sit this evening, push beyond your previous limits, as an athlete would do. See in your mind's eye that edge of irritability, of restlessness, and move beyond it.

# Dealing with Difficult People

*Humans are not simply beings who manipulate their world. They are capable of reading the message that the world carries within it, that is written in all the things making up the world. . . . They are so many symbols of a great alphabet, an alphabet in the service of a message inscribed in things. The message can be described and deciphered by anyone with open eyes.*

Leonardo Boff, Brazilian liberation theologian

There may be some people in your life who cause you trouble at every turn. With these people, whether friends, family members, or coworkers, it's "my way or the highway." You have tried reasoning with them, you have tried yelling and screaming, and nothing works. When a relationship becomes unmanageable after all strategies fail, it is okay to dial back your involvement with the difficult person. You can do this without being mean, and you can still maintain minimal contact in most cases. You need not feel guilty for preserving some sense of sanity.

This evening, someone may be getting under your skin. Notice that in your head there is usually a mental loop that you play, of the wrongs committed by this person, the complaints, the sour expressions, etc. Let go of the loop, and let go of the irritation. Keep playing that mental script, and the annoyance remains. You don't have to stop the loop entirely, just step back from it. See it as a construction.

# Words, Images, and Feelings

*Just as the Twig is bent, the Tree's inclined.*

*Alexander Pope, English poet*

Thoughts, whether they come in the form of words or images or something foggier than that, are tendencies. They are not inert but have real consequences and follow one upon the other. The next thought follows along in the trajectory of the one that came before, and a real direction and momentum can be built in this way, for good or ill. This process cannot be stopped, but mindfulness makes us aware that it is happening. It can help us to see the trajectory of the thoughts, slow down their maddening pace, and move them in a positive direction.

This evening, as you look upon the stream of your own thoughts, what do you notice about them? Take note of words, followed by images and feelings. Do not encourage the internal dialogue: just look at it. Realize that if you can look at this stream of thoughts, you must be separate from it. Sit calmly and watch. See if you can detach from the flow of words, images, and feelings.

# Become the Conduit for Your Own Peace

*Aum! That is infinite, and this is infinite. / The infinite proceeds from the infinite. / Taking the infinitude of the infinite, / It remains as the infinite alone. / Aum! Peace! Peace! Peace!*

Brihadaranyaka Upanishad

If you have ever kept a to-do list, you have probably noticed that only the items at the very top of the list get accomplished on a given day. The rest of the to-do list really becomes something like a wish list or a long-range plan. Rather than berate yourself for not getting to the bottom of the list, honor your own choices and trust that you must have had a good reason for prioritizing what you did. As you trust yourself to make good decisions, your confidence grows, and you can begin to enjoy the process.

This evening, put the to-do list behind you, in the same way that you would put down the map after reaching your destination. Forget about all of the flaws your home may have, and allow it to become your sanctuary, your temple. See the sacred space around you and within you. See the space pervaded by the holy, however you might care to visualize that. See all worry, all anger, all doubt dissolve before the holiness that you now cultivate. Become the conduit for your own peace.

# Getting Into the Devotional Mood

*If with your whole will and mind you are unable to fix your attention entirely on Me, / Devote to this concentration at least a brief period during the twenty-four hours of the day. / Then as long as the mind contemplates My joy, sense pleasures will not appeal to it.*

Jnaneshwari 12:104–16

With our human minds, we don't really know what is the correct philosophy, theology, or doctrine. We are like people trapped in quicksand, looking for a handhold. And yet, amazingly enough, great souls do escape from the quicksand, and they reach out their hands to those still stuck in the mire. What makes these souls great? It is not their intellect or erudition but the way in which they empty themselves and so allow the inner illumination to shine through. They are able to help others because they have passed beyond desire.

Undoubtedly, you already have some guiding lights in your own life, the teachers who have shown you the way. This evening, concentrate on some teaching that you have received; it could be a few verses or lines from a spiritual book. Repeat these words in your mind a few times, until you grasp the meaning without the words. Allow that impression to take you into a devotional feeling. Stay with that feeling and intensify it for as long as you can.

# The Path of Nature: Let It Flow

*Hanumān leaped forward without a moment's hesitation. . . . He was truly a wondrous sight. . . . His eyes blazed bright as lightning, like twin fires upon a mountain slope, like the sun and moon frozen in place. . . . The wind under his arms rumbled and he shot forward like a blazing comet.*

Ramayana, *"Beauty" portion, trans. Arshia Sattar*

We make the mistake of trying to do things with our own power and our own intellect. We forget that the latent powers of nature are far stronger. We will be able to accomplish far more with much less drama if we can just get ourselves out of the way and let the work flow. The ego masquerades as a friend and advocate, but it is actually a great hindrance and limitation. The calm state, the clear state of mind does so much more with ease than the mind so concerned with rewards and praise. All we need to do is look upon God or Nature as the doer and get out of the way. The commentary, the endless second-guessing and hemming and hawing, do not accomplish anything and actually hinder our best efforts.

This evening, do your remaining chores without any commentary: Work automatically and allow things to occur in their own course. Avoid all entertainment. As you sit in meditation, abandon all thoughts of success or failure, doing it right or wrong. Allow your inner intuition to guide you to the deepest and most silent place within yourself. Abandon words and images. Stay in this dark, quiet place until you feel led back to normal consciousness.

# Renouncing Fear

*I must not fear. / Fear is the mind-killer. / Fear is the little-death that brings total obliteration. / I will face my fear. / I will permit it to pass over me and through me.*

"Litany Against Fear," from Frank Herbert's Dune

Fear is one of the major reasons why we skip our practice. We fear missing out on experiences that we might have had in mundane consciousness. We fear what we might learn about ourselves in the space of silence. We have to remember that fear is an excitatory state, that there is a kind of buzz to it. We can be addicted to fear like a drug. And yet, to continue with the practice, we have to renounce fear, to surrender that little jolt of adrenaline that we receive from it. We have to admit that we actually crave fear and then abandon that craving.

As you go into the space of meditation this evening, you most likely will feel that old familiar fear. "I can't stop to meditate," it says; "I have to do this, this, and this." Or maybe fear will raise the specter of some painful memory or flog you with regret. Do not believe in these specters, these doubts. See them as a Halloween ghost, which is nothing more than an old bedsheet moved by the wind. See if you can move beyond fear, to the peace that comes in its wake.

# Mundane or Magical,
# It's All for the Good

*Great is the reward of virtue. The vicious suffer.*

Sri Sai Baba of Shirdi, Hindu saint

Not every day can be a breakthrough day. Not every day will feel super magically awesome. Most days nothing especially fantabulous happens. But the great days, the really special days, are built on the momentum of the completely average Tuesdays. What you do on the normal, boring days makes the magic happen on the amazing days. The hard but really important thing is to keep believing that your efforts make a difference, that not the slightest, tiny effort goes unrewarded. Every cause has an effect, which means that every good thing that you do—eventually—will result in good things happening.

This evening, whether you have had a completely normal, average day or a super fantastic day, give thanks for what you have been able to accomplish. As you settle into your evening moments of quiet, know in your heart of hearts that you are being guided down a divine path of ever greater illumination. Take heart in the ultimate goodness of the universe, and in the divine light within you.

# Go Outside and Play!

*The emotional experience of wonder brings a sense of the fullness of the present moment, the existential now. It dethrones ordinary plans, purposes, and motivations and makes us receptive to our participation in a more general order of life.*

Robert C. Fuller, scholar of religion

We spend so much of our adult lives in the mode of purposefulness, accomplishment, and achievement. Indeed, we come to believe that this is the only way to live, at least the only practical way. So we come to measure things and people by how well they suit our purposes. This attitude becomes a kind of everyday monstrousness. We forget that we can laugh and play and be surprised.

This evening, take a few minutes for play, true play with no other motive. Go outside and lay in a hammock. Talk to your favorite tree or animal. Be foolish. Run in circles. Climb a tree. Blow bubbles. Look for four-leafed clovers. Don't do anything productive or "adult" for at least half an hour. Don't even think about looking at your cell phone. No, you can't just check your e-mail.

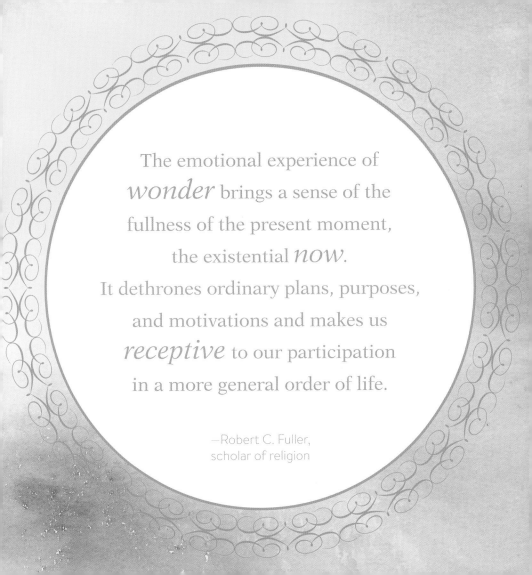

The emotional experience of
*wonder* brings a sense of the
fullness of the present moment,
the existential *now*.
It dethrones ordinary plans, purposes,
and motivations and makes us
*receptive* to our participation
in a more general order of life.

—Robert C. Fuller,
scholar of religion

# A Third-Person Exercise

*All that religious debate comes to is that A's idea is different from B's.
Revelation does not help us because that materially consists in correcting
the ideas of A & B by those of C. If you wish to make your idea of God
nobler, the way to do it is to make your mind nobler, and in particular to
cultivate that noblest part of it which you owe God.*

Aleister Crowley, occultist, founder of Thelema

Emotional states are not very reliable indicators of how things are going in
life. You may feel sad, depressed, or guilty, but that doesn't mean that you
have actually done anything badly or done anything wrong. Sometimes the
emotions just misfire, or sometimes they blow things out of proportion. By
stepping back into the observer stance, watching emotions, thoughts, and
events as they unfold, we can gain a more full and detached perspective
on what is happening.

This evening, as you sit in your meditation space, pretend that your internal camera is panning over your head, as though you were looking down on
your own body from just over your shoulder. Then pull farther back, as though
you were looking down from the ceiling. Then move through the roof (it's
okay; you can see through it) and so on, up into the sky. See yourself as a tiny
speck down below, and then move back down into your own body. Repeat
this exercise when you need to detach from troublesome situations.

# Unforced Forgiveness, Just in Time

*Forgiveness doesn't only resolve our past; it alleviates our fear of the future.*

Kris Carr, Crazy Sexy *author and cancer survivor*

At a certain point in our adult lives, we have to forgive the things that our parents or other elder family members did or did not do for us when we were younger. Then there may be more serious situations of abuse or neglect where forgiveness does not come so easily and counseling may be necessary. In these cases, do not force yourself to do something you are not ready to do. The important thing is to loosen the hold that the past has on us so that we can go out and live in the moment and build new, positive memories. If we hold onto those negative things from the past, the strain can cause mental and even physical illnesses.

This evening, mentally forgive that member of your family who did something wrong to you. Hold the inner intention of forgiveness for the entirety of your meditation session. If you cannot forgive this person (*and it is completely okay if you cannot*), make a promise to yourself that you will (*again, when you are ready*) get professional help, for your own sake and not necessarily for the perpetrator. It is time that the wounds from the past no longer hold you back.

# The Transition to a Nonviolent Society

*Nonviolence can be a way of life. And Nonviolence can be a strategy. But for powerful, long-lasting change, Nonviolence as a way of life is the strategy. Nonviolence is an active and powerful way to build a better world. It involves this fundamental understanding: We and everything are connected. Nonviolence means living your life sincerely supporting those connections.*

*Nonviolence United*

If we want to stop seeing the headlines of mass shootings, military interventions, and general bloodshed and death, we have to begin building an overall culture of peace. We cannot glorify violence in our entertainment media and then act surprised when someone picks up a gun. We cannot practice blind patriotism and then be surprised when our country invades another country. We have to start at the ground level, teaching our children about nonviolence and abstaining from harm in our personal lives as much as possible. We need to teach resistance to racism, colonialism, classism, and misogyny to ourselves and others. Society is a big ship that needs a lot of room to turn around, but we can do it, one degree at a time.

Search your heart and mind for traces of bloodlust. Maybe this bloodlust is not overt, like the desire to fight or kill someone. Maybe it is more like a vicarious desire for excitement that comes from watching violent acts. Inquire into the root of this craving without chastising yourself in any way. See if you can find the source of the attraction to violent rhetoric and violent images. If you can understand this desire in yourself, you will be better situated to understand it in others.

# Appreciating Boring, Ugly, and Plain Spaces

*When Dante and other poets speak of muses, they are not perpetuating myths about magical influences. Rather, they are employing the poetic device of personification to convey gratitude for the inspiring influences that imbue their work with purpose and significance. They are grateful for the opportunity to express something that is deeper, more authentic, and more timeless than the ideas they manufacture during their less inspired moments.*

Todd Thrash, psychologist and coauthor of "Inspiration and the Creative Process"

Plain spaces and ugly places have their proper role to play in the life of the spirit. They reduce external distractions and inspire the life of the mind. They force us to confront what we really appreciate in life. They lead us to inquire within. While it might be counterintuitive, one can find illumination in a back alley while gazing upon broken glass and cigarette butts. Mindfulness is as available in the city streets as it is in the Himalayan snows, for those who know how to discipline themselves.

This evening, as you sit down to meditate, think of the most boring possible place in your life. Maybe it's your cubicle at work, the waiting room at your dentist's office, or in line at the Department of Motor Vehicles. Picture yourself meditating there, in the least conducive space, in the place least likely to appear on a yoga calendar. If you can turn these places into sacred space, then your willpower will be unstoppable.

# Competition and Cooperation

*American culture is a purgatory of longing. Ambition's measures*
*are immeasurable. Our ardent desire for rank or power is*
*continually quantified by titles, prizes, promotions, evaluations,*
*hours billed, grades on papers, firsts, longests, mosts, bylines,*
*batting averages, bank accounts, books published. . . . We are*
*told that our reach should exceed our grasp. But, like Icarus,*
*only after we have fallen from the sky are we retrospectively*
*seen as having flown too close to the sun.*

William Casey King, author and historian

We all have a tug of war happening inside ourselves all the time. We want to be rich and famous, but we also want to live peaceful, meaningful lives. We want to be the very best at something, but we also want to belong to our communities. Competition and cooperation sit warily side by side, gaining the upper hand in turn. Can we stop this cycle? Only by seeing that the individual and society are part of the same greater unity. At a higher dimension, they are one and the same. "I" and "we" are moments, perspectives on the primal flux called nature, God, or Mother.

This evening, do you find yourself wanting to distinguish yourself and be unique, or do you crave nurture and belonging? Wherever you are on this spectrum this evening, it is well and good. Just observe your need for success and your need for communion. When you find your place on this continuum, see if you can view the two poles of extreme individualism and extreme communalism as nondual. Find a place of comfort and surrender with the desires and drives within your personality. Accept these desires and drives without identifying with them.

# Fearless Examination of Belief

*Human beings cannot endure emptiness and desolation; they will fill the vacuum by creating a new focus of meaning. The idols of fundamentalism are not good substitutes for God; if we are to create a vibrant new faith for the twenty-first century, we should, perhaps, ponder the history of God for some lessons and warnings.*

Karen Armstrong, scholar of religion

God is not really a gender-neutral term in the Western theologies and philosophies. What we call God is a barely disguised, masculine sky god, clumsily purged of pagan associations, plucked out of a decayed pantheon and held up as having always been One. A cursory reading of the Abrahamic scriptures and the history of these traditions will show it to be the case that God has only violently and with great acts of internal and external repression become One. There is nothing at all wrong with belonging to one of these traditions, but it is absolutely necessary to be mindful of the history of the ideology to which one subscribes.

This evening, take a look at your most cherished beliefs. Look at the ways in which these beliefs have caused you pain and suffering. Then also look at the pleasures and privileges that your beliefs have brought you. Hold up your beliefs to the internal light and make a fearless inquiry into their true nature. See what you want to keep and what you want to discard. Whatever you decide is well and good, only hold onto your integrity.

# Hot and Cold, Weary and Hungry

*The highest teaching in the world is silence. There is nothing higher than this.*

*Robert Adams, jnana yogi*

Know that when you are tired, when you are hungry, when you are hot or cold, you will be more prone to be irritable and complain inwardly. So at these times, you have to be more vigilant in mindfulness and give others more latitude, more forgiveness. It will help a little bit to do things more slowly and deliberately. Remember that it is better to break a fast and be kind to your brothers and sisters than it is to fast and be cruel to them. We all have different strengths at different times, and we need to be aware of our limits.

Great yogis have been able to cope with extreme heat and cold. You can practice this without putting yourself into personal danger by just going a little beyond your comfort zone. Try sitting outside for meditation rather than inside. Leave your comfortable socks or sweater off. Sleep for a night on the floor. Just make sure to give yourself recovery time, and remember that none of this is worthwhile if it causes you to act harshly toward others or feel pride within.

# The Right Teaching

*Through the vistas of the past the voice of the centuries is coming down to us; the voice of the sages of the Himalayas and the recluses of the forest; the voice that came to the Semitic races; the voice that spoke through Buddha and other spiritual giants; the voice that comes from those who live in the light that accompanied man in the beginning of the earth—the light that shines wherever man goes and lives with him forever—is coming to us even now. This voice is like the little rivulets that come from the mountains. Now they disappear, and now they appear again in stronger flow till finally they unite in one mighty majestic flood.*

*Swami Vivekananda, founder, Ramakrishna Math and Ramakrishna Mission*

The right teachings appear when you are ready for them. You don't need to look very hard, only listen to your heart, to the inner guide. The wrong teachings, when seen through the inner guide, will appear cold and lifeless. The right teachings for you will appear warm and glowing. If you learn to listen to this guide, you will be spared many wrong turns and dead ends. Your path to illumination will be shorter as you learn to trust in your intuition. You will receive hidden guidance, just because you were willing to ask for it and wait for it.

Get in touch with your inner guide this evening by living in a slow and silent manner. Do nothing extraneous. Work diligently but with no haste or aggression. Above all, pay attention. If you can live in this way for long enough, you will begin to receive nudges about the right direction for your life. As you follow these nudges, one at a time, a transformation will begin to take place in your life. Do not try to measure this change: Just take one step at a time.

# The Return of Joy

*When the lower and higher aspects of the Self are well churned together, the fire of knowledge is born from it, which in its mighty conflagration shall burn down all of the fuel of ignorance in us.*

Atma-Bodha

The stages of life, the chapters of life, amount to new adventures into the unknown. Watching a baseball game as a kid is different from watching a baseball game as an adult, which is different from watching a baseball game with a child or grandchild. Same activity, completely different experience. It requires courage to enter a new chapter, to go into the unknown, even if nothing much appears to have changed externally. We all face the unknown every day, but we become more acutely aware of this fact at key transitions and milestones in life. Most of what we take for granted transforms into something else, then fades away. Realizing this, we find freedom.

This evening, you may be struggling with some transition in your life. Observe the inhalation, the exhalation, and the two retentions (inner and outer). Note that as your breath goes through different phases, so does the moon, and so does your own life. Your joy may be occluded for the moment, but that does not mean that it is gone. As the breath returns, as the moon waxes, so does your joy return to you, as cycles return within cycles.

# Reborn in the Breath

*Between the banks of pain and pleasure the river of life flows.*
*It is only when the mind refuses to flow with life, and gets stuck at*
*the banks, that it becomes a problem. By flowing with life I mean*
*acceptance—letting come what comes and go what goes.*

*Nisargadatta Maharaj, Advaita guru*

Western societies, and really most societies in the world today, don't afford much time for the spiritual search. And so we launch young people into the world with big plans, yes, and often much education, but without really allowing them to get acquainted with themselves and the inner life. So they go into the world and they achieve big things but without really knowing what they are doing. This leads to emotional wreckage, bad relationships, all because of a lack of understanding or clarity about basic priorities. They have no idea how to center themselves, how to find that calm place, so they have nowhere to go in times of trouble.

Perhaps you started life on a crash course, with loads of debt and failed relationships. Regardless of how things have gone in the past or how bad they may be now, this evening offers you an opportunity to begin anew, to put the past to bed. This evening, with each exhalation, let go of another aspect of the past. With each inhalation, allow new beginnings into your life. You need not think about the meaning of it all or examine the thoughts: just let this transition to new life happen beneath the level of conscious thought. Trust that you are being reborn in the breath.

# Offering Love at a Distance

*Prayer is not only for times when we find ourselves wounded or broken; it is also a practical skill for everyday life. Your answers may not come in lightning bolts, but during every stormy challenge or sunny opportunity, prayer can renew your mind and transform your world.*

Samuel Patrick Smith, writer and editor

Most monotheistic religions have an idea of intercessory prayer, that you can pray on behalf of someone else to improve a situation at a distance. The Asian philosophies don't have this exact idea, but adepts in these traditions can manipulate cosmic forces, called prana, chi, or kundalini, and spirits or gods may be invoked in order to achieve similar effects. Other traditions believe in the phenomena of remote viewing and telekinesis. We do not yet have a unified theory for how all of this works, but there is a large body of evidence of strange coincidences coming from vastly different metaphysical theories. I tend to think that we should do whatever works, even if it amounts to a kind of enhanced placebo effect.

This evening, take a look at the situations in your own life, particularly those that cause you or someone you love distress. Choose and see if you have exhausted every option for what you can do materially to improve the situation. If you have done so, mentally offer up the situation to your idea of a higher power, within or without. Try to fully surrender the situation and sit in silent expectation for the remainder of your meditation time.

Prayer is not only for times when we find ourselves wounded or broken; it is also A PRACTICAL SKILL FOR EVERYDAY LIFE.

Your answers may not come in lightning bolts, but during every stormy challenge or sunny opportunity, prayer can renew your mind and TRANSFORM YOUR WORLD.

—Samuel Patrick Smith,
writer and editor

# Living in the Body
# Without Guilt

*Within this earthen vessel are bowers and groves, and within*
*it is the Creator: Within this vessel are the seven oceans*
*and the unnumbered stars. The touchstone and the jewel-*
*appraiser are within; And within this vessel the Eternal*
*soundeth, and the spring wells up.*

*Kabir, Indian mystic poet and saint*

As long as you have the body, you have pleasure and pain, and, with them, craving. But these, in themselves, are not a problem. The dharmic traditions do not condemn pleasure: only being governed by pleasure. We should not feel guilty because the body wants what it wants, because it does its thing. The mind, too, has its attachments, wants to create master plans, find patterns, and be useful. We just want to stand back and watch the mind and body. Even this observer stance is not the goal, but it gets us closer to the goal, the blissful state beyond identification with body and mind. We should count ourselves lucky to have bliss every now and then, to be able to see beyond immediate concerns and glimpse eternity.

This evening, you may be experiencing guilt over something you did today or left undone. If it is something small, go ahead and take care of whatever is bothering you. If it can't be simply remedied, look at the bigger picture. You are not the body, and you are not the mind. You are nature and the cause of nature. You are beyond this place and time. Even now, all things are coming to fruition and completion. Make yourself light, a tiny leaf buoyed by a mighty river.

# Expectations and Surprises

*There are no lessons between teacher and student / in a market*
*of bliss. / Since She owns the actors, the stage, and the play itself*
*/ who can grasp the truth of the drama? / A valiant devotee who*
*knows the essence—he / enters that city.*

*Ramprasad Sen, Bengali poet*

The practice of detachment from the fruits of action, as taught in the Bhagavad Gita, is actually pretty important to the practice of meditation or mindfulness. If you go into the practice thinking, "I'm going to be walking on clouds," or, "I'm going to learn how to read minds," there's a real danger of disappointment when the expected results do not materialize. Indeed, mindfulness might make practitioners more aware of problems they didn't know they had. (*Oh, I'm an alcoholic. Oh, I'm kind of mean to people.*) It's important to just be open to the experience, *whatever that might be*, without expecting some sort of cosmic reward.

This evening, what expectations do you have of your practice? Go ahead and name to yourself what you hope to get out of meditation and mindfulness. Surrender these expectations one by one. Be open to the idea that perhaps something else is waiting for you, something you might not have expected. Move deeper into silence and wait there. You are completely safe and well: The insight only comes when you are prepared for it.

# That *Truman Show* Feeling

*The mind has been scattered. It wanders among various objects, which are impressions in our minds. The mind has been divided, and thus mental energy is dissipated. Very little energy is left for the accomplishment of the real ideals in life. But gradually we learn by concentration how to withdraw the scattered forces of the mind and how to focus them upon the chosen ideal.*

Swami Prakashananda, founder and Acharya, Chinmaya Mission of Trinidad and Tobago

When people learn that you practice meditation, they will be watching you, to find out if there really is something to all this mindfulness business. You may come to feel like a representative or sample of sorts. Try to remember that your practice is your practice. Do the mantras, sit in silence, and let the results take care of themselves. The transformation will happen if you just do the practice. You don't have to try to be inspiring to others; that will happen naturally. You don't have to practice your beatific smile in the mirror.

Do you ever have the feeling that you are *on stage*? Like you are the star character in your own TV show? The feeling is quite common in our oversharing society. Some people find the sensation addictive, and others find it to be deeply upsetting. To minimize this feeling of being watched, start with several rounds of deep breathing. Then remember the interconnected nature of all existence, that we are all aspects of the Divine Mother, or, in other terms, all manifestations of the same cosmos, interconnected and interdependent. This will minimize the feeling of separation, of being in the spotlight.

# The Resonance of Things

*What we have forgotten is that thoughts and words are conventions, and that it is fatal to take conventions too seriously. . . . As with money and wealth, so with thoughts and things: ideas and words are more or less fixed, whereas real things change.*

Alan Watts, philosopher

Learning, the true knowledge that really sticks, happens through doing. It would be impossible to learn how to ride a bicycle by reading a book about it. When the Wright brothers built their first planes, they couldn't test them by making sketches. It is the same with mindfulness: We need the practice and not just the theory. The reading and study is all well and good—and very important—but we should not stop there. We have to go ahead and try mindfulness in all aspects of our lives, when sitting still and while working, while chanting and while going to the grocery. With practice, the teachings begin to make sense. Without practice, the books are useless.

Choose an object as the focus of your meditation; it could be a photograph, a flower, a mala (rosary), an apple, or pretty much anything. Note that this thing is not the same today as it was yesterday. It will not be the same tomorrow. It is not static and changeless, even if it is made of stone. Things, then, are not inert but change according to conditions in ways appropriate to their nature. Things are doings, verbs, resonances. Keep working on this exercise over the coming days.

# The Regular People
# (Who Run the World)

*The knowledge which stops at what it does not know is the greatest.*

*Zhuangzi, Chinese philosopher*

We should never look down on the regular people in society or idolize the rich and famous. The celebrities and politicians, the financial speculators, the military generals—none of them actually make the world work, although they might think that they do. The most important people in any given organization do not have a big, long title or work in the corner office. They do not get paid a lot of money. We should be more mindful of these everyday people, who labor mostly in anonymity, who keep our societies running. We should collectively learn how to better appreciate those who just do an honest day's work.

This evening, mentally give thanks for the people in your life who make things work. It could be the mechanic who works on your car, an administrative assistant, the truck drivers who bring products to the store, the farmers who grow food. Think of how lost you would be without them. Let your heart be filled with gratitude, and make sure it shows the next time you encounter a regular person just doing his or her job.

# The Wild Snake of Inspiration

*Anger and depression and sorrow are beautiful things in
a story, but they're like poison to the filmmaker or artist.
They're like a vise grip on creativity. If you're in that grip,
you can hardly get out of bed, much less experience the flow
of creativity and ideas. You must have clarity to create.
You have to be able to catch ideas.*

*David Lynch, American filmmaker*

Inspiration is like a wild animal, a snake who doesn't want to be caught. The creative person grabs ahold of this wild snake and tries to corral it, if only for a moment or two. The snake escapes every time, but the writer, the teacher, the artist comes away with its discarded skin. The shed skin of the snake is not the snake, but holding it up to the light reveals the pattern of its scales. A book, a poem, or a song is like that discarded skin; it points the way to inspiration but is itself a faint impression of a longed-for ideal that remains wild, untamed.

Has a snake crossed your path this evening? Do you have an inspiration that you are trying to corral into a manageable form? Spend some time this evening setting pen to paper, ink to canvas, fingers to instrument. See if you can exercise that inspiration in concrete form. If you fail, take heart: The history of art and literature is just a long record of failures to describe that ineffable something that resists categorization.

# Sitting with Pain

*If an experience is overwhelming you, break it up into its parts, and keep track of them as they arise moment by moment. Often the separate parts are quite manageable individually, hence the aggregate experience loses its power to overwhelm you.*

Shinzen Young, meditation teacher

Your interest in mindfulness and meditation is itself already a desire to improve your life and ultimately the world. You have inaugurated a search for deeper meaning and purpose and a greater connection to those around you. That in itself is worth noticing and worth congratulating. This path of spirituality is long, difficult, and winding, so it is worth taking stock of how far we have come, to gain strength for the climb ahead. You have done a great and courageous thing by opening your heart and mind to this gift of the present, when it would be so much easier to shut down, to avoid getting hurt again. Your openness will bring many wonderful gifts in your life, and yes, also and necessarily, great pain.

Perhaps you have faced some pain today, emotional or physical in nature. This evening, do not build scar tissue around that pain by layering it with commentary. Let the pain just be there, naked and bright. You do not need to *do* anything with the pain this evening. Just observe: do not explain it away or medicate it. Do not feel sorry for yourself: just be there with the pain, your companion.

# Subduing Aggressive Thoughts

*Anger is built on a lower foundation of fear,*
*which rests on a still lower base of fixed beliefs or ideas.*

*Jeffrey Brantley, psychiatrist*

Nonhuman animals kill, but they do so in order to survive. Only human beings kill for sport or for some imaginary idea. Only humans have conducted mass killing, so we should not think that animals are somehow inherently inferior. We should, rather, learn from them; yes even morally. By and large, they do not take more than they need; they bear conditions patiently. They fight but only when necessary, usually not to the death. Cooperation is widespread among all animals. It is not the animal nature of humanity that is dangerous but the power derived by the human mind, especially the unguarded use of language and symbols.

Perhaps you would never physically attack another person, but take a look at your internal dialogue this evening. As you breathe deeply, do you see aggressive, critical, vengeful thoughts arising? If you try to combat these thoughts directly, you will only strengthen them. Give them more space by releasing the ego nature. As you let go of these thoughts, they will become less powerful. Give up your ownership of thought, as though these ugly thoughts belonged to someone else.

# The Undercurrent of Sound

*Be a fearless artist today—not someday.*

Guillaume Wolf, visual artist

We may wish for more money, for more power, because we think that if we had more of these things that we could make the world better (see the trap there: if I just had a little more . . . ). But what really matters is how we make use of the resources—the time, the money, the power—that we already have. Take a piece of cardboard and draw something beautiful. Tape it to the wall: You have already improved the world more than most titans of industry. Pick a flower and give it to someone. Play a musical instrument. Dance. Unfurl the most beautiful secret inside you.

As you sit in your meditation space this evening, listen to the rhythms around you. You may hear your breath, your heartbeat, the subtle sounds of thought. You may hear a bird outside, singing the evening prayers. You may hear the sounds of the HVAC in your house. Using these sounds as your starting point, merge into the surroundings. Blend into the body and then into the subtle body. Become one with the undercurrent of sound.

# Sacred Space and Time

*The Kingdom of Heaven is like the yeast a woman used in making bread. Even though she put only a little yeast in three measures of flour, it permeated every part of the dough.*

Matthew 13:33

We spend so much of our lives in purposely lifeless spaces, painted business beige or plastered with advertisements. Give yourself the luxury of a little space of your own. It doesn't have to be a whole room; a corner or a windowsill will do. Put into your sacred space the beautiful things that inspire you. It could be a picture of your guru or spiritual teacher, a divine figure or saint. Put the shells that you find on the beach, a rock that you found on a hike. Burn a candle or lamp; light some incense. This will help you to set aside sacred space and time. When you dedicate one space and time to the divine, it transforms all space and time.

Everything that you require is right here in front of you. Do not exhaust yourself by running to and fro: Concentrate your mind into one point, centered on the brow. As the thoughts come and go, plow through them, as the bow of a ship cuts through the water. Just let them pass over you. Maintain an active, ready mind, expectant with the desire for peace. Let all other desires fade. Hold to your purpose firmly and eagerly.

# A Glimpse of the Moon

*The one priority I have . . . is to keep it simple. To keep it as perfectly bare and simple as possible. And get it down.*

Townes Van Zandt, songwriter

We must keep working at liberation, the disentanglement of our minds from the troubles and the pleasures of life, the purification of action to the barest essentials. We get stuck and then must get unstuck again. We have to nurture the caring part of ourselves without needing so much from others. This is difficult, this caring without attachment. Letting people go their own ways while also helping them as we can. We have to keep working at this, even when we are tired of working. The price for realization is high, but it helps us to avoid the sorrow of not striving, not trying.

This evening, you may wonder if the effort of mindfulness is worthwhile. It is easier to live in the tunnel of constant distraction. For just a few minutes, put down everything and pay attention. See if you can catch a glimpse of the moonlight outside. Listen for the sound of crickets. See the streetlights outside, people walking their dogs. These little observances, these glimpsed routines, root us to our places, to our lives. It helps to glimpse the world outside of our own minds for a few seconds, to stop thinking so much about our own plans.

# More Than the Bare Minimum

*We must not exert ourselves nor relax our efforts too much or too little.*

*Aristotle, Greek philosopher*

"Give more than you take" is the unofficial motto of my guru, Swamiji. This simple phrase is illuminating, because it is not complete self-abnegation. It recognizes that we all have needs, and yet it also calls us to go beyond our ordinary complacency. It allows us to take what we need but also burn away some of the negative karma that holds us back in life. It applies to nearly everything, to all of the communities to which we belong—our work lives, our spiritual lives, our home lives. It acknowledges that we have to contribute something of our own effort and resourcefulness.

This evening, are there areas of your life in which you are basically allowing others to carry you? Are there areas where you are not doing your fair share? Where you are doing the bare minimum? If you can identify these areas, you may need to do some rethinking of priorities. You may have some confusion in that area of your life, or you may need to push harder.

# Gauging Consciousness

*The sage rejects extremes, rejects excess, rejects extravagance.*

Tao Te Ching

In the older cars my family had when I was a kid, we had to check the oil and the coolant all the time. The dipstick went deep down in the engine and made an oil mark so that you could tell if you needed to add a quart. If you did not check the engine enough, it would overheat and you would find yourself walking down the side of the road. Our minds are the same way: They can overheat and stop functioning. So we have to check the temperature at which we are operating; take stock of the state of consciousness. The coolant, the oil, in this case is mindfulness and meditation, which allows us to keep calm and collected in any circumstance so that we do not suffer breakdowns.

This evening, as you look on your own consciousness, are you cool and collected or stressed and overheating? Breathe deeply into the areas of your mind where you need the most help. As you observe the thoughts, perhaps there are some that are more insistent and stubborn. Direct the breath (and any mantra that you practice) toward these thoughts. If they still won't go away, continue to just observe without getting entangled.

# Loosening the Either/Or

*We cling tenaciously, not merely to believing,*
*but to believing just what we do believe.*

Charles Sanders Peirce, American philosopher

We tend to get caught in false dichotomies in life. *Either I work myself to death, or I will starve. I have to be either scientific or religious. I am either conservative or liberal. Everything must either be true or false.* This kind of categorical, excluded-middle thought process is encouraged in Western society, but it doesn't obtain in the real world, which has a lot of nuance and complexity. We can express our individuality in many ways, *even contradictory ways*, without sacrificing our core principles. The universe is big enough to accommodate divergent perspectives, and we don't have to decide on an either/or basis. Each perspective has a certain truth to it, so long as it doesn't claim to have a monopoly on truth.

This evening, do you find yourself taking a hard-line stance on something? Can you find even a single instance in which your perspective might be wrong? Take a step back and *see the whole*. See how divergent perspectives, even those that might be violently opposed to each other, can be incorporated into a larger harmony. See how perspectives that seem to be opposite actually reinforce one another. See how enemies need each other.

# The Cave of the Heart

*First one small circle; then a larger circle; then the whole universe!*

Yogaswami of Sri Lanka, Hindu master

As devotees, as spiritual aspirants, our job is mostly to be there and do the work. Whether we are chanting or doing silent meditation or studying scriptures, we just have to bring our attention to bear on the task at hand. That's all. Simple and yet difficult. Just make it to the meditation space and sit. Be present. Everything else will come. And then we take that same *bhava*, that same devotional attitude, and apply it to everything in life. We do everything with mindfulness and build it into the fabric of our lives, so that it becomes more natural. We take things slowly and appreciate life and each other. We become more caring, and that's how it goes.

This evening, you are worrying your poor mind with so many thoughts. Set them down, dear one, set them down. Enough for today. Carrying your spine as straight as you can muster, following the chariot of deep breathing, enter into the cave of the heart chakra. Let the golden effulgent light embrace you: Allow it to fill you while the celestial singers intone the ancient song from before the world began. See how color and sound, texture and light combine here in the heart, where all things begin and end. Here is the cosmic egg that gave birth to the universe. Here the big bang, here infinity.

First one small circle;

then a larger circle;

then the whole universe!

—Yogaswami of Sri Lanka,
Hindu master

# Synchronization

*You must say, "I will." And you must say it in thought and in deed, not only now in word. And henceforth never for a moment must your purpose change, but your constant intention must turn everything you touch into line with it.*

Ernest Wood, theosophist

If the average person were to step up to the plate at a major-league ballfield, the ninety-six-mile-per-hour fastball coming off the pitcher's windup would appear to hit the catcher's glove instantaneously. It would be nearly impossible for the beginner to hit it. But for the professionals, who have spent many years in training, the impossible becomes possible. The swing is perfectly timed with the ball leaving the glove so that it connects with the stitched leather sphere hurtling through space. The distinct crack of contact with the wooden bat electrifies the entire stadium and the television audience. So all of the great human feats arise from the perfect synchronization of mind, body, and surround.

As you sit down this evening, you likely have a fog of preoccupation clouding your mind's eye. Draw conscious attention to the breath, and direct your interior gaze to the point between the eyes. Become extremely attentive and alert. Observe any pain that you might have, and feel the blood running through your veins, perhaps in the neck or head. See the outlines of your body as outlined by sensation in the skin. Fill this luminous outline with the breath and merge into the breath.

# Sad Stories We Tell Ourselves

*At root, self-pity is a stalling device. It is a temper tantrum,*
*a self-inflicted drama that has little to do, ever, with the facts.*

Julia Cameron, author

Everyone has a sad story, a victim story, a story of being wronged. Nearly every such story has at least a grain of truth in it. The world is full of unscrupulous landlords, creepy relatives, and evil corporations. But while we must be compassionate with others and ourselves, we shouldn't let the sad story become a self-fulfilling prophecy. We shouldn't let the sad story become a defining feature of our identities. At this point, the sad story becomes truly limiting. Mindfulness practice cannot erase the wrongs of the past, but it can call our attention to the stories that we repeatedly tell ourselves. We can learn to say, "There I go again, feeling sorry for myself."

Perhaps you can think of a sad story that you tell about yourself, perhaps a time when you were injured or harmed in some way. Perhaps you blame a relative, a friend, a company, or even God. When this story arises in your mind, you can just notice and acknowledge it. You might say to yourself, "I see what you are saying, but I am not going to go down that path now." Then return to the mantra, to the breath, or to some more positive thought.

# Silencing Your Internal Conversations

*The body, mind, and emotions all need to be moving in the same direction, and in this sense one needs a strong integrated personality. . . . Integrated personalities attempt to solve problems, while fragmented personalities evade them.*

Robert Altobello, philosopher

The ventriloquist throws his voice to make a dummy talk in the old-time comedy acts. The comedian then gets to be two people at once, and the dummy can do the dirty work of insulting people and telling off-color jokes. Maybe the reason that you don't see this act much anymore is that it's just not that funny and really kind of mean. But we all have a sort of evil twin inside, and we all do this act with ourselves: being nice with one voice and mean with another. Every single person has a split personality of sorts, because consciousness has never been unitary. The mindfulness practitioner recognizes all of the voices, whether *good* or *bad*, as fictitious in a sense. We try to return to the root of consciousness, before language, where there is bare awareness.

Do you have a mean voice and a nice voice inside your head? Or a know-it-all voice and a mock-modest voice? Perhaps you have different personas for different situations. See if you can recognize two or three of your internal selves. See if you can recognize the tone of voice of each. The next time they start jabbering, just say (in your schoolteacher voice), "I hear you, but that's enough." See if you can lengthen the silences between internal conversations.

# Dullness and Dryness in the Spiritual Life

*My eyes have become swollen by constantly blowing the fire to keep it burning.*

Sri Sarada Devi, Hindu saint

After many months of daily meditation, you may find that things begin to get a little stale. The mantra or the relaxation that once worked for you now falls flat. You hit a plateau where your regimen is neither very challenging nor very rewarding. Try to do something to celebrate the rhythm that you have achieved. Perhaps you can take a day off from work or go on a retreat. Maybe you can buy yourself a new mala or meditation cushion. Then try something new, like a more difficult practice from your tradition. If you are having trouble finding something, ask your spiritual preceptor.

When the dull, dry feeling comes over you, don't run away from it. Treat it just like you would any other thought that arises in consciousness. Sharpen your observational skills. Notice the stream of words and images associated with this feeling. Notice the bodily sensations. See if you can tie the dull feeling to any particular life events. Spiritual journaling may help, but by all means, avoid self-criticism and excessive analysis. Shred the journal pages when you are finished with them. Push through the dryness and find the solace on the other side.

# Meditating in All Circumstances

*Acceptance in the mindful context means that even when the unthinkable happens, we honor our self and our experience with dignity and kindness. Rather than turn our back on our own suffering, we treat ourselves as we would a beloved friend.*

Heather Stang, thanatologist and yoga therapist

The only times when you shouldn't meditate in a formal sense are in the case of major life upsets and extreme fatigue. By major life upsets, I mean a major argument with a loved one or a major illness or death. At these times, it is more important to simply be with your loved ones. You may be able to do some *japa*, or mantra repetition, but that is all. By extreme fatigue, I mean what they call in the South being "dog tired." You actually can't stay awake. Sometimes it is better to just take a nap and try again later. You may have a dreamless sleep, which is considered yogic, or you may dream something interesting or revelatory.

You also don't need to be rigid, like a soldier. See if you can find a nice balance between being too lax or too severe. Be skeptical of any thought that might be arising in your mind tonight that you are inherently lazy or some other moralistic term. Go beyond your comfort level, but you do not need to torture yourself.

# Resolve, Effort, and Grace

*Chronos is the world's time. . . . Kairos is intimacy with the Real. . . .*
*We exist in chronos. We long for kairos.*

*Sarah Ban Breathnach, spiritual writer*

God and guru work according to their own timetables. You cannot predict insight or enlightenment. You can only make your life more conducive to the realization that you wish to achieve. So think about what you think will be conducive and what will not. A firm resolve must accompany sincere effort, without which nothing will happen. Believe in the proximity and possibility of your release. And then do the work, patiently and confidently, not trusting in yourself but in the ultimate reality, however you might choose to name it.

This evening, as you do your meditation, probe the secret depths of your own fear. Perhaps you hold back, because you secretly fear the freedom that would come from liberation. You may not want to reorder your life or let go of various compulsions and addictions. And yet, at the same time, dare to push into that unknown country, where you build a new life for yourself and others. Dare to know that place where your dreams become reality.

# Building a
# Community of Seekers

*The possession of Knowledge, unless accompanied by a manifestation
and expression in Action, is like the hoarding of precious metals—
a vain and foolish thing. Knowledge, like Wealth, is intended for Use.*

The Kybalion *by Three Initiates*

Enlightenment is costly, very difficult, demanding great sacrifices. But the typical mindset of humanity also demands great sacrifices. We have to constantly sacrifice our time and attention, our hopes and aspirations, upon the altar of distraction and consumption. So we will sacrifice one way or the other: The only choice is the direction that will guide our willing and acting. Will we continue to be entranced by the dreams foisted on us by consumer culture, or will we dare to dream new dreams and enact new visions? The clear-minded community of enlightened souls is waiting to be born, but we must first take the reins of our own power and begin to build this community. It will come with great effort, and then all at once, like a bolt of lightning.

As you fill your stomach, side ribs, and chest with the vital breath, also fill the community of seekers with the light of inspiration and peace. Wish for the well-being of all, and treasure in your heart all those who are working for peace and justice. As you strengthen your own heart and mind, will that others might also be strengthened.

# Basic Goodness

*As great as the infinite space beyond is the space within the lotus of the heart. Both heaven and earth are contained in that inner space, both fire and air, sun and moon, lightning and stars.*

*Chandogya Upanishad*

You have before you a few ordinary moments of quiet, but treasure them. Life is made out of such moments. At the golden hour just after sunset, the shadows lengthen, and the birds give a last few furtive chirps in the trees. Work slows to a crawl and then stops. Cars line up on the highways, and the streetlights flicker on. People walk their dogs and sit down to the evening meal. Notice everything that happens around you, and, in your attention, pronounce a blessing. All of this is good and as it should be. All of this has its place in the culmination of all things.

You may be harboring guilt and doubt in your heart even now. Suppose you did something that you consider wrong today. Know that sin or wrongdoing is not your true nature. You might make mistakes—everyone does—but treasure in your heart the knowledge of your basic goodness. All this basic goodness to expand and fill you. Let it burn away the doubt and confusion. Let it overflow into your every thought and action. Harbor no ill will toward anyone or anything. All of this is good.

# Waxing and Waning Phases

*If you bring forth what is within you, what you bring forth will save you.*

*The Gospel according to Thomas*

Everything happens according to cycles, waxing and waning phases. The great saints also went through periods of greater or lesser fervor, only their phases would be undetectable to us, so small were their oscillations. If we are to make improvements in our practice, we must learn to make the best use of the low periods as well as the high ones. When we are feeling unmotivated, it is okay to perform chanting or meditation in a routine manner. This builds the energy for when the next upcycle comes. Time is a gift, and we should not throw any of it away.

This evening, you may not feel like doing any meditation or conducting yourself with mindfulness. Muster as much dynamism as you can. Perform meditation as a duty: It's perfectly okay to not feel enthusiastic all the time. Smile at least a little bit. Breathe deeply. Ask that the malaise be taken away, but commit to the practice even if it remains. It is okay to live in the space of forlornness; everyone feels it from time to time. Let this feeling be a sense of solidarity with humanity.

# Kites on the Wind

*As the river flows, from out of the formless void*
*arises the greatest of great realities—a simple smile.*

Bernadette Roberts, Christian mystic

Kites, borne aloft on the wind, wheel and dip, their happy colors displayed to all. They do not fly of their own power but by the wind that propels them. They have no light of their own, but the sun shines through them. They can be dragons or airplanes or superheroes, with nearly infinite combinations, their streamers dancing merrily. We crave power and light that we do not have; we forget that power and light are available freely to all. All that we have to do is find our true nature and the uplift happens automatically. The divine light shines when we release control, when we are borne aloft on the wind of the spirit.

You have enough intelligence, enough time, enough talent, enough money. You have everything you need right now to reach the heights of realization. As you sit down this evening, concentrate on making yourself available to the universe. Open your mind and heart to inspiration. Let go of the dark and heavy thoughts, and become a conduit for pure light. Feel the great uplift within your heart, and let it take you higher each passing moment.

# The Power of Thought

*The thought "who am I?" will destroy all other thoughts, and like the stick used for stirring the funeral pyre, it will itself be burnt up in the end. Then, there will be Self-realization.*

*Ramana Maharshi, Hindu saint*

Thought can bring the past back to life or call future realities into being. It can govern the unfolding of society and bring low the rulers of humanity. The written and spoken word arises from the storehouse of language within each language user. We govern the thoughts not out of some misanthropic skepticism, but because we have come to realize the great power of words and ideas. Because thought has so much power of transformation, we have to be very careful with it, knowing that we are working with something volatile. We have to bring forth the very best, not just for ourselves but for our shared world.

This evening, trace the words flowing in your mind back to their source. Inquire of yourself, peeling back the layers of consciousness until you can't go any further. Sit there and watch the thoughts arise, ever inquiring about their origin. When you have become habituated to this inquiry, let go and allow only the attitude of questioning and inquiry to persist. If you lapse into reverie or dialogue, call your attention back.

# The Matrix
# of Possibility

*One can call all simple substances or created monads*
*entelechies, for they have in themselves a certain perfection; . . .*
*they have a sufficiency (autarkeia) that makes them the sources*
*of their internal actions, and, so to speak, incorporeal automata.*

G.W. Leibniz, German philosopher

Think of a mathematical point: You will see that it is nearly impossible
to picture accurately. Then think of space as composed of such points.
Then see each point as storing a possible value, such as a number or a
color. See each point as having infinite potential. This will provide the
way to contemplation of God (or universe) as infinite hospitality, as om-
nipotence, in the sense of complete possibility and openness (emptiness
if you like). Then you will see that the image of God as judge is quite
impossible, as God is the space of unfolding potential, the complete and
utter acceptance of the forms that the divine matrix takes. Since we
have been given this limitless space of unfolding potential, it is incum-
bent upon us to make the world as beautiful and just as we can make it.

Feel for a few moments the awesome weight of freedom, and with
it, responsibility. You can shape your world however you see fit, your
mind however you see fit. You can and do create your own world every

day. The only restriction placed on you is that you will have to live with your own creations. Make the mind good and its creations good, and you will live in complete beauty! Injustice and ugliness are just bad dreams: Change the dreamer and change the dream.

# Do Your Best

*Art is whatever you can get away with.*

Marshall McLuhan, author and communication theorist

It is not my job to consider whether I win awards or promotions, salary increases or bonuses. It is not my job to consider whether people like or dislike me. It is not my job to consider whether my work is well-received or broadly panned. My job is to simply do the work, whether in my spiritual life or in my temporal affairs. I can only control what I can control; other people will do what they will do. This simple truth, found in the Bhagavad Gita and other spiritual writings, can be extremely freeing. Fretting about outcomes only leads to anxiety, while concentrating on effort leads to peace.

This evening, do not evaluate yourself based on dollars and cents earned or words of praise garnered. Think only of doing your duty to the best of your ability. Where duties conflict, go with the one you consider to be highest and closest to your mission. Where you have faltered, resolve to do better tomorrow. Having made this self-inventory, let it go. Set it down and simply be. Put your mind into that clear state that gets you through the trying times in life.

# Out of the Defensive Crouch

*One can very easily live happily in life provided he understands these three things: learn to give, learn to love, and learn to be selfless.*

Sri Swami Rama, founder, Himalayan Institute of Yoga Science and Philosophy

Love saves us time and time again. We curl into a defensive crouch after some major life catastrophe and vow to never love again. Loving again might be foolishness, but it is a divine foolishness, a life-giving foolishness. As social animals, we cannot live entirely alone. Even the hermit atop a mountain is fed by an entire village and lives to inspire them. As we love others, we feed ourselves, and so the world goes. Money does not make the world go round: love does.

Maybe you have been hurt in some aspect of your life. Maybe a relationship fell apart, or you were fired from a job. Maybe an unscrupulous person took advantage of you financially. Look there inside your heart and mind. See the hurt, the reluctance to begin again, the defensive crouch. This evening, can you begin to think about starting anew? You think it might go badly again, but you do not *know* that it will go badly again. Entertain, for a minute, the possibility that something beautiful might come into your life.

One can very easily
live happily in life
provided he understands
these three things:
learn to give,
learn to love, AND
learn to be selfless.

—Sri Swami Rama,
founder, Himalayan Institute of
Yoga Science and Philosophy

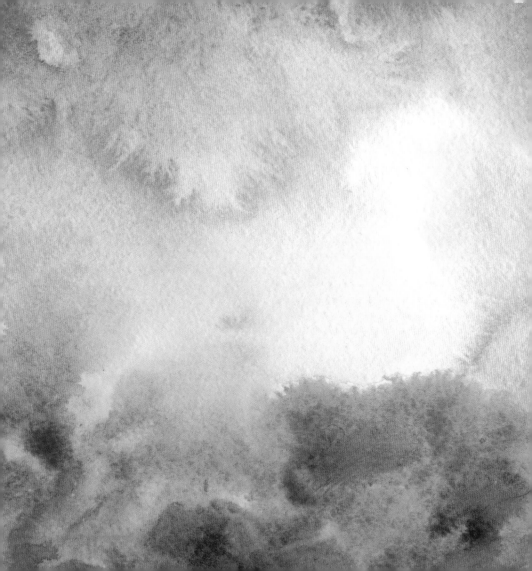

# Increasing Self-Understanding, Not Objectivity

*We as humans are psychosomatic phenomena.*
*It is absolutely impossible to separate our physical body*
*and environment from our mental and emotional states.*

Atreya, Ayurvedic scholar and healer

Objectivity will always be an impossible ideal for us as humans because we have no way to abstract an illusory rationality from our earthly, situated lives. We have feeling and relationships, commitments and beliefs, and we cannot simply throw all this away in order to view the world as detached observers. The best we can hope to do is to be clear about what we believe and who we love, to acknowledge our thoughts and feelings, to become, in short, more self-reflexive. And that is exactly what mindfulness helps us to do: know ourselves more fully so that we can understand our own motivations and be responsible for them.

Are there parts of yourself that you have never fully owned, have never fully acknowledged? Say here this evening: *What am I missing? What am I refusing to acknowledge about myself?* Sit in silence, expectantly holding open this question. After a period of silence (however much you can muster), return to the question and see if you have an answer. If nothing comes, repeat this exercise over the coming days.

# Openness to Others

*Not only are You freedom, but You also will me, You arouse me too as freedom, You invite me to create myself, You are this very invitation.*

Gabriel Marcel, French philosopher

There can be a social anxiety that fears from the other a kind of annihilation, a fear that if I welcome you, I will negate myself. It is true that sometimes others ask of us more than we are willing to give. And yet, at the same time, serving others is also a form of self-expression. If I work to meet your needs, I also draw out of myself something that would not have otherwise existed. That is true no matter what form the service takes: cooking a meal, writing an article, or pruning a hedge. Mutual service calls forth the artistry lying just beneath the surface, makes the unseen come into the light.

In what areas of your life do you withhold service to others? It could be on the job, in your relationships, or just in casual interaction. Know that by withholding service to others you may also be decreasing the vitality of your own life. Open yourself to the people who share your life with you, if only now, in the silent space of meditation. See your heart opening, your physical posture opening, your facial expressions opening. Cultivate a willing attitude, and let go of the guardedness of the past.

# New Visions of God

*Humility is a virtue, not a neurosis. . . . A humility that freezes our being and frustrates all healthy activity is not humility at all, but a disguised form of pride.*

Thomas Merton, Trappist monk

There is a dark place that one goes through in the spiritual life, especially if the transcendence and kingship of the divine are emphasized over the immanence and motherliness of the divine. A false narrative is created in which the devotee feels she must destroy and debase herself before God. This self-flagellation never actually destroys the self, but it increases the ego nature in a subtle form of self-congratulation. *See how committed I am! See how much I am willing to endure!* This pattern reaches no logical conclusion and only ends through an act of surrender.

Perhaps you have tortured yourself in the past due to a religious commitment or due to a misguided notion about God-as-taskmaster. Perhaps bad experiences from the past have stunted your spiritual growth. This evening, allow yourself to imagine God as a supportive mother, as a dear friend, as a beloved animal. Imagine God as your favorite and most comfortable T-shirt, your favorite song, your best friend. Imagine that you have the freedom to imagine the divine, and do so.

# Front Porch Philosophy

*There does not have to be a single basic stuff. Materialism and idealism are not the names of warring tribes but the names of half-truths, neither of which can really be swelled into a comprehensive system.*

Mary Midgley, *English philosopher*

The demand for purity of belief and completeness of metaphysical explanation can certainly create beautiful abstract systems of philosophy, but these sterile systems bear little relation to the messiness and uncertainty of life. So the best philosophers have, at one time or another, always looked to poetry and metaphor rather than descriptive prose to paint a picture of reality. We resign ourselves to the fact that the curve will never touch the y-axis, that analysis will never fully arrive at a complete picture of the world. So we put down pen and paper and sit on the porch. We rock awhile, drink some lemonade, and listen to the cicadas in the pines.

You may be going in circles in your spiritual life because you have been looking for the perfect doctrine, the perfect description of the world-as-it-is. Let go of the need for a perfect system and attend to whatever is right here with you. Don't think so much about what is correct and think more about what helps. Sitting here observing, watching the breath, watching the thoughts. This doesn't necessarily lead to an elaborate metaphysical system, but it does loosen the closed heart and mind. It does make the load lighter.

# The Span of Love

*With few exceptions, we are not hermits or loners. We are social creatures. And, at the level of our creative efforts, we seek teachers, masters, and our fellows. Who else speaks our language, who else can understand, who else can help us over the high, rocky passes and through the valleys of our own shadows? It is too scary and hard to go it alone.*

*Judy Reeves, writer and writing coach*

Fruit flies only live for a month or so. Dogs live maybe ten or twenty years. People live anywhere from a few days to a hundred and twenty years. It is not the length of life that matters but the quality of love and relationships that we put into our days. If we have love and been loved in return, our lives have not been for nothing. Even if we love imperfectly and are, in many ways, incapable of receiving love, the little bit of love that we allow ourselves will be enough. A day or a hundred and twenty years, that little bit of love will be enough to see us through, to make it all worthwhile.

How much love can you pack into your time on earth? How much love can you allow yourself? How much love can you give? How much can you receive? Can you open the floodgates a little bit this evening? Can you be a little less cautious and a little more optimistic? Meditate on love this evening: Try to see it and understand it. Bring it into your life a little more completely. Allow it expression in concrete ways toward the people and animals in your life.

# Decompartmentalizing

*The bond that attaches us to the life outside ourselves*
*is the same bond that holds us to our own life.*

*William Barrett, American philosopher*

Silent meditation, *japa* recitation, study of scripture, chanting—these are all techniques for realization; they are not realization itself. We should be willing to set aside the tools once the realization dawns, and we should recognize the danger of the techniques becoming ends in themselves. I should give a generous allotment of time to these practices, but I should also be willing to help my neighbor when the time arises. I have to do the practice, but I also have to do all the mundane things of everyday life. Nor should I wish to be excused from the everyday difficulties that ordinary people face.

You may sometimes develop a bifurcation or compartmentalization of your life into spiritual and worldly tasks. This evening, blur the lines between what you consider mundane and what you consider spiritual. As you are folding laundry, make that into a spiritual practice. As you are reciting mantra, make that into manual labor. Completely merge these aspects of existence so that they become one for you: live into this synthesis.

# Ancient Wisdom

*To return to the observance of the rites through*
*overcoming the self constitutes benevolence.*

Confucius

There is an arrogance of popular culture that encourages a certain posturing in which we pretend to have the answers, to have the right style, to stand alone and unique as individuals. To show deference to traditional modes of thought, to ritual and ceremony, is thought to be outmoded and backward. The best things are thought to be those that came about in the last five minutes. The worst things are thought to be those from long ago. We can, without committing the logical error of the appeal to authority, still recognize that our ancient ancestors surpassed us in many ways. They thought more deeply about the proper relationship between human beings and nature, about the way to lead a satisfying life, about the way to be a good person. We scoff at such things only at our peril.

This evening, find a good translation of an ancient text (Eastern or Western) and read one chapter, slowly and deliberately. Whatever text you choose, allow the reading to read you. Let the text speak to your own life and the issues facing society today. Also be aware of the strangeness of the text, the ways in which things were just completely different in the author's time. See if you can pick a key phrase that can become a focus for a few minutes of silent meditation.

# Let Go and Let God(dess)

*Witnessing the destruction of confusion, the Gods*
*experience extreme joy! See how many contemplations,*
*prejudices, and attitudes from which we have*
*been freed! Having given up all the difficulties, all*
*the thoughts, the very ego itself, to Kālī, the mind*
*experiences the utmost peace and delight!*

Swami Satyananda Saraswati

Living in the twenty-first century can be very scary. Our societies undergo continual shocks from environmental depredation and economic uncertainty. Our personal lives are often filled with conflict. The technologies meant to give us amusement cause a meaningless ennui. We are left adrift. Fortunately we have a sacred thread running through our lives, a thread of scripture and story, chanting and song, meditation and mindfulness. We do not have to face the daunting future alone in this age of darkness. For the Divine Mother swallows all of our doubt and confusion, all of our need and longing. She becomes the mother for us and saves us with her demon-destroying weapons of consciousness.

Say a few hundred repetitions of your favorite mantra to the Divine Mother. See how the sound reverberates through your mind, how it fills your chest cavity. Picture all of the thoughts being reduced to ashes by the Divine Mother. See how she clears the battlefield and leaves only peace in her wake. Give up all thought to her and surrender to her mighty weapons. She will see you through the storms of life and set your feet on solid ground.

For more information and further reading, see
http://anahatachakrasatsanga.org/bibliography/

•